The Difficult Hire

Titles in the CAREER SAVVY Series™:

Anger and Conflict in the Workplace

100 Top Internet Job Sites

101 Hiring Mistakes Employers Make . . . and How to Avoid Them

Recruit and Retain the Best

The 100 Best Web Sites for HR Professionals

The Difficult Hire

Savvy Interviewing

The Savvy Resume Writer

The Difficult Hire

Seven Recruitment and Selection
Principles For Hard to Fill Positions

Dennis Doverpike
Rhonda Tuel

Impact Publications
Manassas Park, VA

Library of Congress Cataloging-in-Publication Data

Doverspike, Dennis
   The difficult hire : seven recruitment and selection principles for hard-to-fill positions
Dennis Doverspike, Rhonda Tuel.
      p. cm.
   Includes bibliographical references and index.
   ISBN 1-57023-137-0
   1. Employees—Recruiting.   I.Tuel, Rhonda.   II. Title.

   HF5549.5.R44D68 2000
   658.3' 111—dc21

                                                                    00-031913

Publisher: For information, including current and forthcoming publications, authors, press kits, and submission guidelines, visit: *www.impactpublications.com*

Publicity/Rights: For information on publicity, author interviews, and subsidiary rights, contact Media Relations: Tel. 703-361-7300 or Fax 703-335-9486.

Sales/Distribution: For information on distribution or quantity discount rates, call (703-361-7300), fax (703-335-9486), e-mail (*difficult@impactpublications.com*) or write: Sales Department, Impact Publications, 9104 Manassas Drive, Suite N, Manassas Park, VA 20111. Bookstore orders should be directed to our trade distributor: National Book Network, 15200 NBN Way, Blue Ridge Summit, PA 17214, Tel. 1-800-462-6420.

Layout and Design by C. M. Chapman

Contents

Dedication

This book is dedicated to our spouses,
Ida Doverspike and Byron Rossi.

Acknowledgments

Dennis Doverspike

I would like to start by acknowledging my coauthor, Rhonda Tuel. The ideas contained in this book were the product of many years of hard work, trial-and-error, and debates over the best way to present abstract concepts. A great deal of patience and understanding was required on Rhonda's part, and so I thank Rhonda for her tolerance and her tenacity.

My wife, Ida, and my sons, Dan and Tom, had to endure my unusual work habits and hours. In addition, Dan and Tom had to put up with my holding the computer hostage for long periods of time. I would also like to thank my wife's parents, Mary and Louie Reisner, and my parents, Mary and Dan Doverspike, for their support during this period.

I would like to thank all of the graduate students, undergraduate students, and other faculty, who have collaborated with me on research and projects over the years. The following individuals deserve a special note of thanks for helping to review sections of the book: Winfred Arthur, Jr., Alana Blumental, Linda Brown, Ida Doverspike, Carolyn Lees, Mary Hogue, Karl Jaeger, Jennifer Ludwig, Rosanna Miguel-Feruito, James Porter (who also provided expert advice on grammar and structure), Sheila Rutt, and any other anonymous or long forgotten reviewers or contributors. I would like to thank the University of Akron for financial support, as portions of this book were completed during a sabbatical which was awarded by the University.

A final thank you goes out to Ron and Caryl Krannich at Impact Publications for supporting our vision. Without their assistance, we could have never translated our thought, theories, and experiences into the pages of this book.

Rhonda Tuel (Rossi)

Among the many fine individuals and organizations who helped make this book possible, I would like to express my gratitude to Richard L. Jebber, President of Mattress Warehouse, who gave me the freedom to recruit in unique and creative ways, although I was just starting my career. I would also like to express my thanks to Diebold, Inc., for giving me the autonomy to utilize and train with my innovative techniques, while actively recognizing my successes. I would like to extend a special thanks to those Diebold associates who helped me to develop and grow professionally: Robert Stockamp, John Gotch, Kevin Nadzam, Art Roebken, and David Evans. I would also like to thank the Professors in the Graduate Department of Counseling and Human Development at Walsh University for my solid education in counseling techniques and theories.

On a personal note, I would like to extend an extra warm thank you to my friend Amy Fuller who has supported and inspired me more than she will ever know. Finally, my love and deepest thanks to my fiancee at the time I was writing the book, and now my spouse, Byron Rossi. Thank you for showing me that dreams do come true.

1

The Art and Attitude
of Recruiting

This book focuses on the art of recruiting. It's about developing a particular attitude for becoming a more effective recruiter. Unlike other books on this subject, this one is not intended to serve as a technical reference for recruiting. You will not find, for example, details on how to prospect for candidates, negotiate a salary, or write up a no-compete agreement. Although we do present a series of steps for effective recruiting, our steps are a means to an end. For the recruiter, the end is to develop a proper attitude toward the hiring process. For the job candidate, the end is a perception that a job with the organization is valuable and that getting the job is a significant accomplishment. For the organization, the end is to create an appropriate climate for recruiting.

The Difficult Hire

More specifically, this book deals with the art of recruiting for hard to fill positions, or the difficult hire. Successful recruiting for hard to fill positions requires recruiters, whether by profession or training, who must understand the psychology of the job candidate. The recruiter needs to understand why people take jobs with organizations and what makes the difficult hire possible. Most important of all, the recruiter must believe that he or she can make the seemingly impossible become a reality and, over time, change the very nature of the organization by hiring high quality employees.

Intended Audience

This book was written for anyone who seeks answers to problems encountered in hiring and recruiting. It is intended for human resource managers and business owners who need to understand why they fail to attract successful and desirable candidates, even though they try to recruit according to the rules. It is also intended for line managers and supervisors who assist in recruiting and selection; they need a quick guide or handbook to handling problems.

Although the book is based on our theory of vocational behavior and our knowledge of the scientific literature, it was not written for an academic audience. It's especially written for those on the front lines of the recruiting wars— those who are trying to recruit the difficult hires. The book is designed to be useful regardless of whether one is a small business owner, a supervisor, or the Vice President of Human Resources at a major corporation.

An Attitudinal Approach

This book is primarily about recruiting. While we do discuss selection, we examine it within the context of the recruiting process. Thus, our emphasis is on selection as part of the recruitment of the difficult hire. Selection, in and of itself, is a very critical, important process. Indeed, you'll find many fine books dealing with personnel selection, such as *Hiring Great People* by Kevin Klinvex, Matthew O'Connell, and Christopher Klinvex, and *Applied Psychology in Human Resource Management* by Wayne Cascio (see the Selected Bibliography at the end of this book for complete references). But very few books attempt to integrate selection into an overall philosophy of recruiting.

We are not major proponents of the view that recruiters must sell the job and organization to the recruit, especially if that involves a hard sell or if it involves making selection as pain-free as possible for the job candidate. This is not to say that the sales analogy cannot at times be useful, especially when applied to writing the position advertisement or to closing the hire.

However, people value what they believe is hard to get. That is basic human psychology. Effective recruiting requires making the job and the organization something to be desired. A mark of successful recruiting is when the new hire can brag to their friends and family about how proud they are that they got a job with your company. Of course, this process works at peak efficiency when both the recruiter and the recruits truly believe that the job and the company are to be valued and that the new hires have proven their mettle to the company.

The basis of our philosophy is rooted in human nature and perception. Recruiting becomes much easier, especially for hard to fill positions, when recruiters create a perception of value and a climate of achievement. A climate of achievement is created by making the job something to be valued and by placing the job candidate in a position where he or she has to work hard in order to earn the job. By managing perceptions, the recruiter can make the difficult hire a possibility.

But make no mistake here. By "managing perception" we do not mean to imply that you should be dishonest with yourself or the job candidate. Intelligent, competent job candidates see through dishonesty. In order to convince others of the value of the job and the company, you, the recruiter, must first become convinced of the value, or at least the future value, of the job and the company. Thus, the basic principles presented here are intended to provide a means of reshaping the recruiter's attitude as well as the attitude of the job candidate. As a recruiter, it is important that you believe in yourself, the job, and the company, and then communicate this attitude to the job candidate. Accordingly, the goal of this book is to change your attitudes and fundamental beliefs.

We prefer to take a scientific approach to human resource management issues. Unfortunately, very little scientific research exists in either the human resource management or industrial psychology literatures on the topic of recruiting (but for an exception, and an excellent review of the academic literature, see *Recruiting Employees: Individual and Organizational Perspectives* by Alison Barber).

A similar dearth of literature exists in the applied press. There appear to be more books advising job seekers on the job search than there are for companies on how to recruit. Recruiting simply seems to be a topic which receives less attention than other human resource management topics, although there are signs that the situation is changing with additional books appearing aimed at the human resource professional and readings also available on related issues such as legal concerns and behaviorally based interviewing (for a comprehensive handbook on the technical side of recruiting, see *Recruiting, Interviewing, Selecting and Orienting New Employees* by Diane Arthur).

Please be forewarned that we are not lawyers. Unfortunately, in today's workplace, recruiting cannot be conducted without an eye to applicable laws and regulations. We highly recommend that anyone involved in recruiting and hiring be aware of any applicable laws and regulations and seek out legal guidance when appropriate (consultants and law firms offer regular seminars which cover various aspects of equal employment law). Many laws and regulations which apply to recruiting and hiring vary from state to state. Given the importance of legal issues, we include a chapter which deals with an overview of relevant legal, professional and ethical issues. However, we repeat the caution that we are not lawyers and thus we do not dispense legal advice.

Defining the Basics

When we use the term recruiter, we refer to anyone involved in the hiring process who might interact with the job candidate. This includes, of course, the college recruiter, the Human Resource Director, and the Vice President of Human Resources. But, it also can include the small business owner, the line manager, or the store manager. In these days of teams and employee referrals, it can also include the factory worker, the salesperson, or the engineer. Since everyone, and anyone, at some time may be a recruiter, it's important to offer training to all the employees in your organization who are involved in any aspect of recruiting.

Throughout this book, we prefer using the term job candidate, or just candidate, when referring to the person being recruited. We use this term instead of applicant, because, as we explain in Chapter 7, the term applicant has additional meanings, although it does have a more generic, public meaning, a certain degree of caution should be exercised in the use of the term. As a result, we use the term job candidate to refer to that hypothetical person seeking a job, or being sought after, who, we hope, eventually does become a difficult but possible hire.

Users and Uses

The principles outlined in this book have been tested by the authors in practical applications. We have used them as the basis of training programs and in our work with a variety of jobs and companies. Our principles also are timely given recent changes in recruiting, especially the increased use of both the Internet and phone screening in recruiting. We believe our principles are equally applicable when recruiting and interviewing are done over the phone, in person, or over the Internet.

The organization of this book reflects the approach we have used successfully in training. Chapter 2 serves as a basic introduction to the challenge of recruiting for hard to fill positions. Chapter 3 outlines the basic principles of recruiting the difficult hire. Chapter 4 deals with the initial contact between recruiter and candidate. Chapters 5 and 6 present detailed information on the screening process. Chapter 5 covers the areas of identifying the qualities you are looking for in a new hire, minimum qualifications, and testing. Then, Chapter 6 covers the selection interview. Chapter 7 deals with the art of closing or of getting the candidate to commit to the organization. Chapter 8 reviews the topics of ensuring equal employment opportunity and related professional issues. Chapter 9 includes a discussion of a variety of issues which should be of special interest and concern to human resource professionals including the recruitment of members of Generation X, recruiting in the public sector, recruiting by employers of choice, and tips on managing a career in human resources. Chapter 10 begins by discussing the impact that changes in recruitment will have on the organization and then presents recommendations on how to respond to resistence to change from other employees and from managers. Finally, Chapter 11 presents our concluding thoughts, including suggestions on combating relapse.

We have tried to capture the essence of successful training programs we've delivered to managers and other personnel concerned with recruitment processes in organizations. As a result, we have condensed materials to contain what we believe are the essentials needed in order to deal with recruiting for hard to fill positions.

The ideas presented in this book have been developed by the authors over the past 10 years, and in some cases, over the past 20 years. As Scott Adams noted in the appendix to his highly successful book, *The Dilbert Future*, it is often difficult to identify the source of all of our ideas. Many of our theories and arguments are based upon our extensive training and backgrounds in psychology. Due to the nature of this book, we have not used the extensive footnoting style so often found in scientific writing. However, we provide the reader with a link to the technical literature in the Selected Bibliography and also have provided suggestions throughout the book for future reading and research.

This book was written to stand alone as a useful resource for small business owners, recruiters, and human resource professionals. We have also attempted to create a book which could be used by human resource professionals in designing their own workshops or by instructors as a textbook on the art of recruiting. Anticipating such uses, we include an outline or syllabus for a training program in Appendix A, along with copies of several role playing exercises. The whole book should be useful in training programs involving professional recruiters or human resource professionals. However, in training situations involving employees with more limited involvement in the recruitment process, the instructor may find that the next seven chapters and the last chapter, Chapter 11, are the most relevant. Although Chapters 9 and 10 contain material which should be of interest to anyone involved in recruiting difficult hires, these chapters were written primarily for the human resource professional. As a result, the instructor may decide to skip Chapters 9 and 10; it should be possible to do so without interfering with the comprehension or the delivery of the essential content.

Purpose and People

The purpose of this book is to make the difficult hire easier. What follows is a set of principles which we believe are required to successfully recruit, screen, and hire for hard to fill positions.

Please remember that we are not simply trying to exchange knowledge but are instead trying to present an underlying philosophy of the art of recruiting for hard to fill positions. The book should result in changing your basic attitude toward recruiting. We do not claim to be offering any magical solutions; change can be difficult and can also require a lot of hard work. Hopefully, you will come away from this book with an understanding and belief that you can play a major role in shaping the future of one of your organization's most important resources—its people. Over time, you can change the very face of your organization and ultimately remake your company into an employer of choice—where difficult hires become relatively easy.

2

The Challenge of Recruiting for the Hard to Fill Position

In the not so distant past, employers did not worry about having to recruit job applicants and then sell them on taking a job. All a company had to do was put up the help wanted sign or run an advertisement in the local paper, and they could count on a long line of prospective job candidates. The issue was not one of finding qualified applicants, nor even one of convincing them to take the job, but the problem was one of choosing among a plethora of qualified applicants. As a result, employers and human resource management professionals tended to ignore the science and art of recruiting and concentrated on areas such as selection.

But times have changed. Today we have low unemployment (currently estimated at 4%, and for some types of workers and occupations as low as 1%), an aging workforce with a smaller number of young adults, and a shortage of persons with skills relevant to the emerging technology and service sectors. Candidates for jobs do not necessarily stand in long lines waiting to be interviewed by the recruiter. As a result, companies often find themselves with hard to fill positions, or, as we refer to them, *difficult hires*.

For example, consider the case of Chris Spears applying for the position of Customer Service Representative at First Rollins Bank, which is located in an area where unemployment is close to zero and every retail establishment seems to have help wanted signs in the window. First Rollins Bank went through a temporary period of financial instability and had to lay off a large portion of its workforce. However, under new leadership, it has turned itself around and is now one of the fastest growing financial institutions in the region.

First Rollins Bank is currently searching for new employees in order to fill a number of Customer Service Representative positions in their call centers. Employees in the call center receive phone calls and determine whether

8

they can handle the matter or whether it needs to be routed to the technical help desk or some other department. This is a critical position in that as part of the turnaround First Rollins Bank is emphasizing individualized customer service and tries to have employees available at all times to answer questions on accounts, ATM operation, and problems with credit cards. There is also a company mandate that all employees be available to work Saturdays, and new employees are often required to work Sundays, holidays, and on the least desirable shifts. In the past, this requirement of weekend work has turned away a number of potential employees.

The company has determined that the Customer Service Representative must have a high school degree and a minimum typing speed of 30 words per minute. Individuals selected for Customer Service Representative positions must also have a strong work ethic, a record of job stability, a pleasant phone voice, and a friendly customer service orientation. Other requirements include well developed interpersonal skills, a desire for a job involving customer service and customer contact, and the ability to perform other related tasks such as operating a computer terminal. Pat Davis, the Human Resource Director, has reviewed Chris Spears's job application and believes that Chris may be qualified. Pat hopes that she can somehow convince Chris to take the job. Pat knows that her ability as a recruiter will be evaluated based on how well she performs in terms of filling the openings for Customer Service Representatives and that her career in human resources will also depend upon her success in finding qualified candidates for the position. For Pat Davis, this is a hard to fill position and an example of a difficult hire.

When people hear the term *difficult hires*, there is a tendency to think of hiring for a position such as a Ph.D. in polymer chemistry, an expert in the latest computer software, or an international business manager who can speak 20 languages and is familiar with cultural habits throughout the world. Well, those are all difficult hires. However, difficult hires also occur in much less exotic professions. Some examples of difficult hires we have encountered include:

❖ Financial institutions, insurance companies or any retailer or manufacturer trying to recruit large numbers of customer service or call center representatives.

❖ The retailer trying to attract professional sales associates.

❖ Telemarketers trying to recruit large numbers of direct marketing representatives.

❖ The small restaurant owner trying to attract servers and cooks to work lunch hours.

❖ The YMCA or similar nonprofit trying to attract anyone from desk help to fitness instructors with a limited budget.

❖ Any firm trying to fill computer, engineering positions or information technology positions.

Regardless of the reasons that a job is hard to fill, or a difficult hire, the business owner or human resource manager must find and hire qualified candidates for the position. This is where the process of recruiting becomes difficult and has undergone such a radical change. The days of simply putting an ad in the paper and interviewing a line of candidates are over. Job candidates today may send resumes in by mail or increasingly by the web. Companies may rely extensively on employee referrals. More and more companies have moved to conducting a substantial portion of their recruitment over the phone or through the Internet rather than in person. Despite these changes, many positions remain difficult to fill.

The Nature of the Problem

What makes some hires so difficult? Why are some positions so hard to fill? Some obvious, fairly concrete reasons include:

❖ Jobs which require skills which are in short supply, such as in areas of emerging technologies.

❖ The company is in a location where there is a shortage of labor and attracting employees to the area is difficult.

❖ The salary for the job is below market or not competitive.

❖ The benefits are below market or seen as not competitive.

❖ The company has just gone through a well-publicized restructuring or series of layoffs.

The above factors are, of course, important reasons. Unfortunately, they may also be pretty much outside of the control of the recruiter. Furthermore, even in the face of an oversupply of labor, some companies have trouble recruiting. On the other hand, even when faced with labor shortages, other companies' recruiting functions seem to be quite successful. Why, even when faced with similar circumstances, do some companies find it easier to recruit than others? We believe that it is because of additional factors which are basically perceptual and can be altered by the recruiter or the organization. Difficult hires may also occur because:

❖ The job candidate's experience with the recruiter is a negative one. The recruiter creates a negative first impression of the job and the organization.

❖ The job has a negative or a poor image. The job is seen as undesirable due to unpleasant working conditions or undesirable hours.

❖ The company or the industry has a negative image or is seen as undesirable for some reason. For example, some sales areas — automobiles, encyclopedias, vacuum cleaners, insurance —

have a negative stereotype associated with the occupation.

❖ The recruitment process and/or the job itself fails to meet the basic needs of the job candidate.

The positive side of recruiting for the difficult hire is that the four factors listed above are basically perceptual. In that they are perceptual, the recruiter can change or affect the job candidate's attitudes through the application of certain basic principles.

Who Is a Recruiter?

In today's organizations, everyone is a recruiter at one time or another. Indeed, this is a major point you should consider and remember:

Everyone is a recruiter

The manager or supervisor who interviews a potential new hire is a recruiter. The current employee who talks to a friend about the company is a recruiter. Every individual may not be a recruiter all of the time, but at some time in their organizational history they are likely to fill the role of a recruiter. So, it is critical that the human resource management department, or whoever is responsible for recruiting, ensures that everyone involved in recruiting understand certain basic principles of recruiting.

Summary

The purpose of this book is to allow you to make the difficult hire. Some of the factors which create a hard to fill position may be outside of your control. However, other major factors are perceptual and can be controlled by the recruiter. In particular, factors which the recruiter can have an influence over include:

❖ The job candidate's perception of the recruiter.

❖ The job candidate's perception of the job.

❖ The job candidate's perception of the company or industry.

❖ Whether the job candidate perceives that their needs have been met.

We have created a set of seven basic principles and also two related techniques which make it possible to change perceptions and successfully recruit for hard to fill positions. These basic principles are presented in the next chapter.

3

The Basic Principles

This chapter outlines the basic principles of finding the difficult hire. While the rest of the book provides more concrete details on the practical application of these principles, the effective recruiter should always keep these principles in mind. That is, to recruit effectively, you must do more than just know these principles — you must believe in them and apply them to the actions you take during recruiting. The principles presented here are really part of a philosophy of recruiting which should serve as a guide to action.

Regardless of how it occurs, at some point there is an *initial contact* between the employer and the job candidate in which a representative of the company, the recruiter, formally indicates to the candidate that there is a mutual interest. Once the employer finds candidates for the position, they must then screen or select those candidates who are identified as qualified for the job. We refer to this process as *screening*. Finally, once qualified applicants are found, the employer must then convince the qualified applicants to continue through the recruitment process until the point is reached where a job offer is extended. This third part of the process, we refer to as *selling the job*.

The basic principles apply regardless of where we are in the hiring or recruitment process. While we can think of the recruitment process as divided into the three phases of *initial contact, screening* and *selling,* this is an artificial distinction. In hiring for hard to fill positions, all three processes are intertwined and are occurring simultaneously.

Information is also exchanged in at least three ways prior to the initial contact. First, the organization has associated with it a general image. Of course, it is often a negative general image which leads to the problem of difficult hires. Second, the organization advertises for job candidates. Ad-

TECHNICAL NOTE: Since we are approaching the problem of recruiting for the difficult hire from the point of view of the recruiter, we begin our discussion of the recruitment process with the initial contact between the recruiter and the job candidate, where there is an expression of mutual interest. Obviously, prior to this point, information has been exchanged between the company and the potential job candidate. Although the precontact phase is a critical phase, a detailed discussion of this topic is beyond the scope of this book.

vertising may be accomplished through a sign in the window, a newspaper advertisement, or a web site on the Internet (for an excellent discussion of the use of the Internet in recruiting, including Internet-based advertisements, see *The Employer's Guide to Recruiting on the Internet* by Ray Schreyer & John McCarter). Through advertising, the organization does attempt to influence perceptions (a short discussion of the application of the basic principles to the writing of a newspaper advertisement has been included in Appendix B). Third, the job candidate sends an initial statement of qualifications to the employer. This may be a job application, a resume, or a vita (the topic of the initial review of a resume or the prescreen is treated in the Minimum Qualifications section of Chapter 5).

The Basic Principles

The basic principles are:

1. You are the most important factor in filling the job.
2. You must stay in control.
3. Put the company and the job on a pedestal.
4. Perceptions are everything and you can change perceptions.
5. Control the negatives.
6. You must fulfill the individual's needs.
7. Set and keep your standards high.

Basic Principle 1.

You are the most important factor in filling the job. Your approach to recruiting and hiring — initial contact, screening, selling — is the most important factor in filling the job.

You must believe and convert this first principle into action. You, the recruiter, are the most important factor in filling the job. Now, we can hear you arguing with us already. No, it cannot be my problem, it must be the (pick one):

- ❖ Industry's reputation
- ❖ Company's image
- ❖ Job market
- ❖ Salary
- ❖ Location
- ❖ Hours, including weekend and holiday schedules

TECHNICAL NOTE: Research conducted on the recruitment process lends support to our argument that recruiters play a pivotal role in the impression which job candidates receive of the company. There is even a scientific theory, known as signaling theory, which states that experiences during the initial stages of recruitment and selection are taken as representative of the norms of the organization. Job candidates prefer recruiters who are warm, enthusiastic, credible and professional. In addition, job candidates are impressed by a recruiter who is able to discuss how the needs and qualifications of the candidate relate to the job and the organization. Unfortunately, the job candidate's impression of the average recruiter is often a negative one. In part, this may reflect the lack of training, as many corporations either do not offer training or offer only very limited instruction to their recruiters. We recommend that all recruiters receive training and have included a sample agenda for a one-day training program in Appendix A.

In order to recruit successfully for the difficult hire, you must start by believing that **you**, the recruiter, are the most important factor — because you are. You are that job candidate's, or potential employee's, window into the soul of the company. You are the conduit by which they receive information on the job and the company.

It is you who will determine how job candidates perceive the company and the job. If you are positive, they will receive a positive image. If you are negative, they will receive a negative image. If you are professional, poised, and polished, then your company will be held in high regard. If you are casual, dull, incompetent, sloppy, or unimpressive, then your company will be held in low regard. Your attitude toward the company and the job will become their attitude toward the company and job. You want to create a positive climate — a climate of achievement.

Basic Principle 2.
You must stay in control. During all interviews or communications with the candidate, you must stay in control of the conversation.

You need to stay in control throughout the recruiting process. You must control your attitude, the job candidate's perceptions, and the flow of information. If you do not, then there is a high likelihood that you will lose good people and select the wrong people.

Control should be established right from the beginning. In order to maintain and establish control, you must be organized. You must have a plan and follow it. Conversation and communications should be controlled, but not dominated, by the recruiter. The candidate should not dominate interviews, even if they are the one doing most of the talking.

The best way to create and hold onto control is to ask questions. As long as you are asking questions, you are in control. The best types of questions to ask are those which lead to the collection of information on job related behaviors.

Staying in control includes having the candidate commit to continuing with the hiring process as you progress through the various stages. The recruiter should control the process including the arrangement of various meetings and interviews. This is not to say that the recruiter should not be flexible, but the perception should be created that the recruiter's time is valuable and that the recruiter is in control.

Basic Principle 3.
You must put the job and the company on a pedestal.
One of the biggest problems in trying to hire for hard to fill positions is adopting the attitude that the company is desperate and that as a result you will take anyone or that all that is needed is a warm body. Even if there is some reality to that statement, it is the wrong attitude to take. It is the wrong attitude for the employer to take and it projects the wrong attitude to the job candidate. In addition, it causes the very problem we are trying to solve — it creates an environment in which it is hard to fill positions. Who wants a job that anyone can get? The answer is either people you do not want to hire or no one at all.

Try to think of something in your own life that you wanted very badly. Why did you want it? Was it something that was easy to get or hard to get? Was it something that anyone could have or something you had to work for? How did you feel when you were trying to achieve your goal? If you did finally get what you wanted, how did you feel then?

Even for hard to fill positions, the best and correct attitude to take is one where the job candidate has to earn the job and the right to work for the company. You must create the perception that the job is not for everyone and that there are certain standards that have to be met by the candidate in order for the individual to earn the job. The acceptance of any other attitude, or accepting less, is a recipe for disaster and the main reason why so many positions become hard to fill.

This is where perception and candidate psychology meet. The perception must be created and exist within the candidate that this is a job worth having and that it is worth the candidate's time and effort to compete for the job. The recruiter must create a climate of achievement where the right person will work hard to try to be selected for the job and will be proud to tell others that they earned the position.

However, this positive perception must also be the attitude that the recruiter adopts. The recruiter must believe and reflect the attitude that this is a great company and that this is a great job, one which anyone would be proud to have attained. If you believe that you will have a difficult time hiring for your hard to fill positions, then the job candidate will sense this attitude and will also adopt a negative outlook. Your attitude will turn into a self-fulfilling prophesy; if you view a job as hard to fill, it will become hard to fill. The job and the company must be something to be desired; the recruiter must put the job and the company up on a pedestal.

Basic Principle 4.
Perceptions are everything and you can change perceptions.
The previous principle establishes that you must create a positive perception of the company. Perceptions are everything, and these perceptions will drive the decision making process for the job candidate. Unfortunately, and it is especially likely to be true for hard to fill positions, the job candidate may not initially share your perception of the company and of the job. The job candidate may have an indifferent or perhaps even negative opinion of your company and of the job. That is when it is critically important that you understand that you can change perceptions.

As Basic Principle 2 suggests, you must start by adopting the attitude that the company and the job are to be desired. Paint in your mind a vivid picture of all of the positive benefits of your company. If it is helpful, write down a list of benefits or create a short benefits checklist or brochure. Think of the positives. If you start by thinking of only the negatives, then you need to start by changing your own perceptions.

It is possible to try to change perceptions of an employer and a job. Perhaps one of the best examples of this is a television advertisement currently running for the United States Marine Corps. In this commercial, in order to become a marine, a recruit must go through a gauntlet of challenges, including a final battle against a huge, fiery monster. Not only is this an example of attempting to change perceptions, it is also a wonderful example of creating a climate of achievement and illustrates the power of establishing high standards.

TECHNICAL NOTE: Typically, there are only moderate levels of agreement among survey respondents in their ratings of their perceptions of companies. In addition, companies may have a general image and also a separate image as an employer. It is possible that a company could have a positive general image, from a customer's or a stockholder's perspective, and yet still have a negative image as an employer. In a study by Scott Highhouse and associates at Bowling Green University, they identified 15 dimensions which characterized a company's image as an employer. The most important factors were the respectability of the company, hearsay and information from others concerning the company, the product image, and the working conditions and atmosphere. The first two dimensions support our arguments concerning the importance of perceptions and also the importance of communications from friends and relatives concerning the company and the job.

Basic Principle 5.
You must control the negatives.

Okay, we heard you arguing with us before. Sure, it would not be the difficult hire if there were no negatives. If the image of the job and company were completely positive, then recruiting and hiring would be easy, and you would have no need for this book. The only issue would be whether the company could offer a job candidate a large enough salary to attract them away from the current employer, or other potential employers.

However, even with the best of jobs and the best of companies, there are negatives. And so, you must always work to control those negatives. The best way to do this is by concentrating on the positives and by creating a climate of achievement. A candidate who is hard at work trying to earn a job will have less time to dwell on the negatives.

The second method of dealing with negatives is to turn them into positives. In order to become a firefighter, a job candidate must endure rigorous physical testing including dummy drags through darkened halls and climbing aerial ladders. It would be quite rational to see this testing as a negative. However, most firefighting candidates see it as a positive and would be disappointed if they did not have to go through the ordeal of physical test-ing. The demands of the testing session are proof that the job they are seek-ing, firefighter, is one which is worth the spirited competition.

The same event, even working weekend hours, can be seen as either a positive or a negative. It is all a matter of managing perceptions.

Basic Principle 6.

You must fulfill the individual's needs. You must understand the psychol-ogy of the job applicant and work to fulfill the individual's needs, espe-cially their need for achievement.

Why do people make choices? How do they decide where to live, whom to marry, or what job to take? How do they decide how hard to work or whether to do a good job? The science of psychology attempts to provide answers to the question of how people choose between a set of alternatives and also attempts to answer the question of what motivates individuals to work hard in order to obtain various rewards.

Of course, human behavior turns out to be quite complex and difficult to predict. However, we do know enough to set up a simple model which can guide the recruitment process and help us to understand the basic psy-chology of the job candidate.

Behavioral choices, including job choices, are guided by four dominant factors:

1. Past behaviors and choices.
2. The attitudes and reactions of significant others.
3. Abilities.
4. Personality, including one's needs and desires.

One factor which affects choice is a person's past behaviors and choices. Not only does a person's past behaviors and choices affect job choice, it also affects how productive a person will be on a job and how well the individual will fit in with the company, the supervisor and coworkers. Thus, it is critical during the screening process, that the recruiter identifies the qualifications of the job candidate, based on their past behavior and choices, and the degree of fit to the job and the company.

A second factor which affects job choice is the opinions and feedback that the job candidate receives from significant others in their life — their friends, neighbors, family, and spouse. This works in at least two directions.

First, others will give the job candidate their opinions of the company or job. They will tell the job candidate what they have heard about the company and whether they think the job candidate should take the job. The opinions of significant others will play a role in shaping the candidate's attitude toward the job and the image of the company.

Second, the candidate will want to get the reaction of the significant others in their life to the hiring process. After getting off the phone with the recruiter, the job candidate will probably turn right away to a spouse, or other family members, and relay the results of the conversation. In addition to receiving feedback from other, the job candidate will be trying to meet their needs for affiliation and achievement by impressing other people in their life with the fact that someone actually wants them for a job. We all want to be wanted, and we want to tell others that we are wanted.

> **TECHNICAL NOTE:** Research suggests that opinions received from relative strangers, especially current employees of the company, are also given great weight by the candidate in that the information is seen as coming from an unbiased source. This leads to the question as to whether the employees in your organization would recommend the company to others? You might want to consider performing a formal or informal survey with employees in your company in order to determine whether they would be willing to recommend the company, and if not, why not.

A third factor which affects choice is a person's abilities. We use the term *abilities* in a general fashion as encompassing a person's knowledge, skills and aptitudes. As with past behaviors, it is critical that during the screening process the recruiter identifies the relevant knowledge, skills, and aptitudes of the job candidate and the degree of fit between the candidate's abilities and the job requirements.

A fourth factor which affects job choice is a person's personality. Today, most personality theorists rely upon some version of a five-factor personality model. According to five-factor models, the more than 15,000 possible personality related attributes can be reduced to five primary factors. The Big Five personality dimensions are:

1. Neuroticism
2. Extroversion
3. Openness
4. Agreeableness
5. Conscientiousness

Neuroticism is a construct which is similar to a lack of emotional stability or adjustment, except that in some cases it may have a curvilinear relationship to emotional stability (i.e., too much neuroticism or too little neuroticism would both be indicative of a potentially unstable person). A person who scores high on this scale would be nervous, easily stressed out, and would tend to describe themselves as worrying a lot.

Extroversion is the tendency to be assertive, active, and, on the surface, sociable. The person who scores high on this scale would be energetic and seek positions of leadership or influence. This is a highly desired trait in sales personnel.

Openness is a somewhat ambiguous construct corresponding to a general willingness to learn from new experiences. Also, openness is sometimes seen as reflecting intelligence or creativity, both of which could be considered to be aptitudes rather than personality dimensions. However, this factor can also be seen as representing culture. The interpretation of scores on openness is probably the most controversial and hotly debated.

Agreeableness reflects a cooperative and easy-to-get along with attitude, someone who is pleasant and likable. Along with extroversion, agreeableness is also an interpersonal factor and corresponds to sociability. People who score relatively high on agreeableness are also likely to do well in teams and in highly structured organizations.

Conscientiousness corresponds to a person who would be seen as a good worker. Conscientiousness reflects a tendency to be dependable, hard-working, and a person who sets and works to achieve goals. A person who scores high on this scale is also likely to prefer cleanliness and order.

Individual differences exist on these personality dimensions, and personality has been found to be related to job performance and job choice. In particular, conscientiousness is consistently, positively related to job performance for almost all jobs. Personality dimensions are also related to individual differences in need strengths.

An important determinant of a person's personality is individual differences in need strength. Of course, money is a major need. There is no doubt that people are motivated by the financial aspects of employment. However, people do have other needs which they try to fulfill through employment. Three needs, which are particularly important in understanding behavior in the workplace, and also responses to the recruitment process, are the need for:

1. Affiliation
2. Achievement
3. Power

The need for affiliation is the desire we have to associate with and to please other people. People with a high need for affiliation like to be with other people. They have close friends and try to please others. A person high in need for affiliation also seeks the support and approval of others.

The need for achievement is the desire we have to reach our goals. The higher the standards, the more satisfaction we receive from accomplishing our goals. People with a high need for achievement try to attain high standards, exceed the performance of others, and do things well. They are also more likely to establish difficult goals in the first place.

The need for power is the desire to control and manipulate the environment, including other people. Individuals with a high need for power seek leadership positions and take charge of situations. They also enjoy persuading and directing others.

A need can be considered to be a lack or a deficit. For example, when a person is hungry, he has a need for food. If a person is thirsty, he has a need for water. Needs serve to direct behavior in that they lead to the goals which motivate behavior. When needs are not met, the result is a feeling of tension or dissatisfaction. When needs are met, the result is a feeling of satisfaction.

Three of the major needs theorists are Henry Murray, Abraham Maslow, and Alfred Adler, each of whom contributed unique insights into our understanding of human behavior. David McClelland has also contributed greatly to our knowledge concerning the need for achievement. Over the years, psychologists have also developed long laundry lists of potential needs as well as tests for the presence of individual differences in needs (two tests which have been used to measure needs are the *Edwards Personal Preference Schedule* and the *Thematic Apperception Test*).

People may vary in the strength of their needs and there does appear to be a relationship between needs and personality. Thus, some people may have a stronger need for achievement than others. However, situations also lead to the strengthening of needs (a phenomenon referred to as **press**). For example, even if we were not thirsty, upon seeing a nice cold soft drink, we might begin to experience a need to drink liquids. In a similar fashion, some situations create a higher need for achievement than others. In recruiting, and in the organization in general, we want to create a climate or press for achievement.

In the recruitment process, we would argue that the need for achievement is particularly critical, that is why we continually emphasize the need to create a climate of achievement. The two needs, achievement and affiliation, also interact in that it really makes a person feel good when they can tell the people who are important to them (need for affiliation) that they have been offered a job based on a rigorous selection procedure which determined that they were the best person for the job (need for achievement). In being hired for a job, people want to think that they have really accomplished something that very few other people could achieve. This works to satisfy both their need for affiliation and their need for achievement.

How do you create a climate of achievement? You create a climate of achievement by having the job candidate work hard during the selection process. As a minimum, we recommend following a series of *five hurdles* organized as follows:

1. Prescreen and minimum qualifications.
2. Phone screen and initial interview.
3. Standardized testing.
4. Second interview with recruiter or Human Resource Director.
5. Interview with appropriate supervisor or manager.

We will discuss this five hurdles approach in greater detail in Chapters 5 and 6. Along with the use of the five hurdles approach, we recommend using a procedure we refer to as the **Prototypical Career Path** method in developing the qualifications required for successful job performance.

To summarize, to be an effective recruiter, you do not need to have a psychology degree nor read the collected works of Sigmund Freud. But, you do need a basic understanding of the psychology of the job candidate. Four factors that will have an impact on job choice are a person's:

1. Past behavior and choices.

2. Perceptions as shaped by the information and feedback they receive from other people.

3. Abilities, including knowledge, skills and aptitudes.

4. Personality, especially their needs for achievement, affiliation and power.

Basic Principle 7.
Even with hard to fill jobs, set and keep your standards high.

The tendency exists with hard to fill jobs to start to say to ourselves that we will just hire the next person to walk

TECHNICAL NOTE:
We have made the concept of *need* a cornerstone of our basic principles. Although theories based on needs have had a rich tradition in the field of psychology, in the 1970s social and personality psychologists began to turn away from need and personality based theories. During the late 1980's and the 1990s, there was a rebirth in psychology of personality theories. We predict that in the 2000s there will be a similar return to need theories.

through the door. If the next job candidate can sign their name on the application form, then they are hired. Hey, that is human nature and we have all been there. However, we also all know that the likely outcome is that within a couple of weeks, we will be filling that position again, except now, we will have an angry supervisor and be paying unemployment compensation.

An important principle in attracting the difficult hire is to create the perception that the job is valued and important and that the person who fills the job will be valued and important. It is critical to remember, then, that just because a position is hard to fill does not mean that we should adopt an attitude that anyone can do the job. The job will actually be easier to fill if we set, maintain and publicize high standards. Now admittedly, high standards can be relative. High standards for a cashier at a fast food restaurant will be different from high standards for an information systems professional. The basic principle remains the same, however, that by raising the standards a job can become easier to fill with the right people.

Please note, this seventh principle actually wraps up the first six principles. By setting high standards, the recruiter takes control of the process, controls perceptions, and sets the basis for fulfilling the job candidate's need for achievement.

Summary

Hopefully, you can already see where and how the basic principles apply to the recruitment process. As we have said, the basic principles apply regardless of exactly what phase of the hiring process you find yourself in. While we can think of the recruiting and hiring process as divided into initial contact, screening and selling, this is an artificial division. All three processes are intertwined and are occurring simultaneously. At certain points during recruiting and hiring, some of the basic principles may seem to apply more than others. However, it is important that you, as a recruiter, adapt the principles and stay faithful to all of them during the process of securing the difficult hire.

For those who desire even more simplicity than the seven basic principles provide, or would like a simple set of affirmations for the recruitment process, the principles can be further summarized as follows:

I am the most important factor in the recruitment process.

I will stay in control.

I will respond to the needs of the candidate.

4

The First Dance – Controlling the Initial Contact

The initial contact between the recruiter and the job candidate is critical to the overall decision-making process. Indeed, first impressions tend to become lasting impressions that disproportionately influence final decisions. Thus, it is critical that the first impression be managed properly.

While all seven basic principles apply to the initial contact, these four basic principles are particularly critical at this stage:

1. You must stay in control.
2. Put the company and the job on a pedestal.
3. Perceptions are everything and you can change perceptions.
4. Control the negatives.

One of the first contacts you will have with the job candidate is probably by phone. To contain costs, many selection interviews may be conducted over the phone. Therefore, in discussing the first contact, and in providing examples, we focus on situations in which the phone might be used. However, the principles of staying in control apply regardless of whether the communication with the candidate is by phone or in person during an interview.

How to Stay in Control

In any human interaction, basic common sense and social psychology both tell us that the first impression is critically important. The first impression can bias processing of critical information. It is this first impression which will shape the interaction with the other person, in this case the job candidate.

In order to stay in control, you must establish your role right from the beginning of the interaction. You, the recruiter, are in the position of power, so this normally should not be too difficult to accomplish. However, some people do have trouble with the initial stages of the interaction and when dealing with the difficult hire. As a result, at times the power may initially be in the hands of the job candidate.

It is critical that you establish control from the beginning. How can you do this? It is really very basic and simple — start out immediately by asking your questions. Have an agenda or list of questions and follow your format; many companies may even use a phone screening pad, which contains canned questions.

Your plan should be laid out ahead of time and then you should stick to it. If you start to vary from your agenda, you will find yourself giving the candidate an opportunity to interrogate you. The candidate will simply lose interest as you scramble to find the next question to ask or figure out what you are going to do next. When you are asking the questions, you are in control.

We are not saying that you should dominate the conversation. You need to let the candidate talk and respond to your questions. We have seen too many recruiters whose idea of controlling the conversation is really one of dominating the conversation. They end up dominating the conversation by telling stories about their families, or, even more damaging, inappropriate stories about co-workers or the company. This is not control; it is a lack of control. You control the conversation by asking questions, not by giving out the answers or by rambling on about your life. As a benchmark, we would suggest that you let the applicant spend 75% of the available time talking or responding to your questions. That leaves you with approximately 25% of the time to ask questions and communicate other essential information.

If the person is an excessive talker, then keep refocusing the conversation. For example, regardless of your question, the job candidate may try to keep telling you about the terrible supervisor they had on their last job. Let's assume you are responding to Chris Spears, a candidate for the Customer Service Representative job at First Rollins Bank. You might say the following:

❖ *"Well, Chris, I understand that you had a problem with your last supervisor, but still, tell me about three things you did for your company which involved improving company service."*

By making such a focused statement, you show the candidate that you are listening and that you care, but you also refocus the conversation on the job-related information you need to collect.

If you do not maintain control of the conversation, several things can happen, almost all of which are bad. One possible outcome is that you will not be able to ask the questions you need to ask. Another result is that you will not be able to collect the information you need to collect. Most important, you have lost control, and control is one of our basic principles. You have thrown the basic principles out the window. The end result is that if the person would have been a good hire, you will probably lose them and, if you do hire someone, that person could well end up being a poor hire.

In order to establish a climate of control, you must have a plan or agenda and stick to it. Your questions should be thought out and organized ahead of time. Then, you need to establish right away that you will be asking the questions. We have found that a good way to start, after exchanging any initial pleasantries, is to say:

❖ *"I need to get some information from you to see if you meet the minimum qualifications for the position."*

This simple statement tells the job candidate right away that you will be shaping the flow of the conversation. As we will discuss later, it also establishes that there are certain standards which have been established for the job.

Of course, not all candidates will cooperate with your desire to seek and maintain control. After all, the candidate will probably have their own agenda and want to ask you questions about employment matters such as pay and benefits.

What should you do when a candidate starts off by trying to question you or ignores your opening question. One simple solution is to attempt to restore control by trying to use the following opener again:

❖ *"I need to get some information from you to see if you meet the minimum qualifications for the position."*

If that does not work, then, just say politely:

❖ *"If you don't mind, I need to get some information from you, before we begin."*

Make it clear, that your questions need to be dealt with first. You should also indicate to the job candidate that you will allocate time later for his or her questions.

At one time or another, everyone has probably encountered an interviewer who simply read their questions one after another from a sheet of paper. What should be a conversation turns into an inquisition. In order to create the perception of a free-flowing, professional interview, you should make use of **transitions**, which simply involves providing a brief summation of the answer to the previous question combined with a natural segue into the next question. For example:

❖ *"Chris, I can certainly see that customer service is one of your strengths and that you enjoy it. Now that we have talked about your strengths, we will move onto what you perceive to be your weaknesses. Chris, can you tell me about a professional area you see as a weakness and would like to improve?"*

Another example would be:

❖ *"Chris, I think I have enough on your educational background. Education is important, but so is the opportunity to apply that knowledge through applied experience. Chris, could you tell me about your previous experience in customer service?"*

In addition to maintaining control, you will want to establish right away that you are responding to the candidate's needs and that you appreciate the candidate's time and attention.

The candidate should feel welcome and should sense that a certain rapport is developing between the candidate and the recruiter.

Again, simple common sense or basic psychological principles can help us to create the perception that we are trying to respond to the candidate's needs. During the conversation, you should repeat and use the candidate's name frequently. This is especially important in a less personal setting such as a phone call. If the candidate's name is used, it makes the candidate feel more involved, attentive and committed to the conversation. It also tells the candidate that you are interested in them as a person and interested in their accomplishments. Higher commitment will translate into higher show rates later on in the hiring process.

Another basic technique is to utilize key words and information from the candidate's past answers in order to demonstrate that you are sharp and intent on remaining in control of the call. This is what many professionals call **active listening**. Take, for example, these active listening responses in the case of Chris Spears:

❖ Chris Spears says to you *"I really like customer service and want to work with people."*

❖ You reply, *"Chris, you say that you like customer service. That's great. We're looking for people who like customer service. Chris, could you tell me about any other jobs which you have had that involved customer service or working with people?"*

Active listening can be taken one step further by creating a connection between the underlying feeling and core values. For example:

❖ Chris Spears says to you, *"In my last job, I really liked answering people's questions. I liked dealing with customers and helping them fill out forms."*

❖ You reply, *"Chris, it sounds like you get a lot of satisfaction from helping customers, because you really value customer ser-*

vice. Chris that is great, because First Rollins Bank also values customer service."

Note that the recruiter in the examples used the job candidate's name repeatedly. Although, when you read this, it may seem redundant, it serves a purpose because it is much more difficult to process spoken words, especially when the target of the communication is a nervous job candidate. The recruiter has shown that she is listening to the candidate and that she understands that the candidate is telling her about his interest in customer service. Not only is information being collected, the recruiter is also building rapport and a relationship.

If you, as the recruiter, effectively develop a relationship with the job candidate, then the candidate will want to meet with you. The job candidate will want to be offered another interview so that he can sit down and talk to you, the recruiter. The candidate will feel as if he already has a friend, a contact, with the company. This personal bond will make him feel as if he wants to be a member of the company. Furthermore, if the job candidate

---

TECHNICAL NOTE: Research suggests that when people are asked what they want out of a job, the answer will be very different from when they are asked what they believe other people would want out of a job. In other words, you may get a more honest response from a job candidate if you ask them about the opinions or behavior of other people. For example, consider a typical job candidate, how do you think they would respond to the question *"Which is more important to you, challenging work or money?"* Now, how do you think they might respond if asked *"Which was more important to other people you have worked with, challenging work or money?"* In your opinion, which response would be more reflective of the candidate's actual attitude? Very few job candidates will tell you that they are not dependable. However, informative answers may be obtained from the questions: *"Are most people dependable? What percentage of other people do you think are dependable?"*

views you as a friend within the company, then he will be even more receptive to your message — and, hopefully, your message is one which creates a positive perception of the job and the company.

How to Control Perceptions

At this point, it might be wise to go back and review some of our basic principles. Remember, we want to control and change perceptions. The applicable basic principles are:

1. Put the company and the job on a pedestal.
2. Perceptions are everything and you can change perceptions.
3. Control the negatives.

Starting with the initial contact, you must begin to create a favorable attitude toward the company and the job. You must then work to establish and maintain this attitude throughout any interviews in the hiring process.

How does one go about creating the desired perception? We suggest starting with this simple principle:

Assume that the candidate will want the job!

That is right. No matter how hard it is to fill the job, no matter how many candidates you have talked to already — you should adopt the attitude that the candidate wants the job. Adopt it, believe it, and communicate it to the job candidate.

If you have trouble adopting this attitude, then try thinking to yourself:

❖ *"I am engaging in this phone conversation/interview to see if this candidate has what it takes to join this great company! I know that my company has a wonderful reputation in the community and this position is one that many people would like to have!"*

Now, what if your company does not have a wonderful reputation or the position is one which people do not find to be desirable. We believe that as a recruiter, you are in the position to make a difference. Of course, it is not enough for others to believe it. You must come to believe in yourself and your abilities. As a recruiter, you can bring in and hire the types of people that will make the company a great company. Recruiters, for better or worse, are in a very public position. Everyone in the company has an opinion on whether the recruiters are hiring good people or bad. If you hire good people, then other employees in the company will have a positive opinion toward you and will tend to cooperate with you. Remember, difficult hires create a state of crisis for the organization. If you can help to solve the problem of the difficult hire, you will have helped everyone through a major crisis.

In most companies, there is probably no better way to create visibility with management than by hiring good people for positions which were previously seen as hard to fill. If you can hire good people for these hard to fill positions, not only will you make your company a better organization, hopefully, you will receive appropriate rewards including pay raises and promotions. At the very least, people inside the company will know you and your name and will associate your name with the good work that you do in filling positions. As you move up in the company, you will find yourself in the position where you can truly change the company and make it a better place to work.

So, if your company has not quite reached the pinnacle, then say to yourself:

> ❖ *"I am engaging in this phone conversation/interview to see if this candidate has what it takes to join this company that I know can be a great company! I know that my company has the potential to have a wonderful reputation in the community and this position is one that people should want to have!"*

You need to find a way to communicate this message to the job candidate. In that initial contact, do not say:

> ❖ *"I am calling you to see if you have an interest in this position which requires weekends/non-traditional hours, etc., . . . "*

Also, do not say:

❖ *"I am calling you to see if you have any interest in the position of Customer Service Representative"*

Saying either of these statements is a major mistake on your part, because it indicates that you are less than confident that the candidate might be interested in the position. Always assume that the candidate will be interested in the position. Thus, the correct response for our hypothetical human resource director would be:

❖ *"This is Pat Davis of First Rollins Bank. I am calling you to discuss the application you sent in regarding the Customer Service Representative position."*

Successfully managing attitudes and perceptions is the key to recruiting for the difficult hire. To persuade the job candidate that the job and company are desirable, the recruiter and the job candidate must both believe that the job and the company are desirable. The recruiter's attitude must convey to the job candidate the perception that:

❖ This job is on a pedestal and it will take some serious work to get it.
❖ This job and the company are something to be valued and we are not going to hire just anyone.
❖ This job is one that the candidate will have to work hard for and really earn.

Remember, you need to instill a climate of achievement. The candidate is going to have to work and sweat to earn the job.

Keep in mind that this is a two-step process. First, you must adopt the right attitude. Second, you must communicate this attitude to the job candidates. If you can adopt this positive attitude and communicate it to the job candidates, then they will perceive that if they get this job they will have accomplished something very special.

TECHNICAL NOTE:

Research suggests that even though job candidates report being interested in receiving negative as well as positive information, they often fail to process negative information. That is, when presented with negative information job candidates appear to "tune it out." In addition, as might be expected, the more negative information job candidates receive concerning a job the less likely they are to accept the position.

Control the Negatives

In dealing with the difficult hire situation, by definition there are negatives. In order to hire for these hard to fill jobs, you must control the negatives and not allow them to control the job candidate's perceptions. You will have to deal with the negatives and answer any questions from the candidate in an honest manner. However, it is your job to turn the negatives into positives or to turn attention away from the negatives to the positives.

A negative frequently encountered in retail or customer service is work schedules. A new employee in a call center may be expected to work holidays such as Christmas and New Years. Some retail stores require employees to work every Saturday. This negative can be turned into a positive by emphasizing that it shows the company's commitment to meeting customer needs. An example follows:

❖ *"Yes, Chris, you will be expected to work holidays, including Christmas and New Years. However, this demonstrates our company's commitment to meeting the needs of the customer. We believe we must be there for the customer, 24 hours a day, and that means our employees must be there. This is really an opportunity for you and the company to show that we are dedicated to the needs of the customer."*

Notice in the example above how what could be considered a negative has been turned into at least a possible positive.

A question you may encounter which can lead to negative answers is:

❖ *"How many people are you going to hire?"*

Examples of negative or incorrect answers would be:

❖ *"Everyone I can get."*
❖ *"We're always trying to hire for these positions, so if I could find five people, I'd take them all!"*

A simple and effective answer to this question is to respond:

❖ *"My goal is to hire two great (or whatever number is reasonable) candidates in the next three weeks."*

You should not respond with any statement that conveys a message of desperation or creates a negative perception of the job or company. A negative or desperate sounding response will make candidates suspicious about what may be inherently wrong with the position or company. It creates a negative perception. The employee may ask you for more information on what you are looking for in terms of number of people or by what date. In response, the information on the need to select good people can be repeated, including emphasizing the importance of the five hurdles. You may also want to put the important qualifications and basic requirements which you are looking for into simpler language.

If the salary for the job is low or the working conditions are poor, then you need to emphasize the positive sides of the job offer package. Perhaps the company offers great benefits, has great people and does a lot of promotion from within the organization. Many companies and compensation experts recommend emphasizing total compensation or the total value of salary plus benefits plus other less tangible factors. Find the positive aspects of the total job package and emphasize the positive aspects of the total compensation package. As mentioned previously, you may want to create a benefits or positive points checklist.

NOTE: By indicating that the recruiter needs to control the negatives, we are not attempting to encourage you to lie, mislead, or be dishonest. In fact, quite the opposite; we encourage you to be honest in discussing the facets of the job. For example, if weekend hours are required, then right up front, the job candidate should definitely be made aware of the fact that weekend hours are required. The difference is in your attitude toward weekend hours. If you indicate to the candidate that "I do not know why they make people work weekend hours, it makes it tough to recruit employees," then the job candidate will share your attitude. On the other hand, if you point out how weekend hours illustrate the company's commitment to customer service, then, hopefully, the candidate will begin to see the positives.

Controlling the Hard to Control Candidate

Now, perhaps you have agreed with everything we have said to this point but are still thinking to yourself, "Yeah, but no matter what I do, sometimes I will run into someone whom I cannot control, someone who resists control and just keeps talking no matter what cues I give them." Well, if you have really done your job and tried to control the conversation, then one question you may want to ask is whether this is the type of an employee you really want to hire. If the person cannot respond to social cues in the interview, then how will they do in interviews with higher level executives, how will they respond to supervisors and coworkers on the job, and how will they respond to customers? If you have done your job, and still cannot control the contact, then maybe this is not the right person for the company to hire.

Summary

The initial contact is very important because human decision making is overly dependent on first impressions and control must be established from the onset. All seven basic principles apply to the initial contact between the recruiter and the candidate. But the following four principles are particularly critical:

1. You must stay in control.
2. Put the company and the job on a pedestal.
3. Perceptions are everything and you can change perceptions.
4. Control the negatives.

In order to establish control and manage perceptions, you must start by assuming that the candidate wants the job and that the job is desirable. Even if the company or the job is less than perfect or has a less than wonderful reputation, you must believe that as a recruiter you can make a difference.

Whether the first contact takes place on the phone or in person, make sure you:

❖ Start out immediately by asking your questions.
❖ Prepare an agenda or list of questions and follow it.
❖ Repeat and use the candidate's name frequently during the conversation.
❖ Use key words and information from the candidate's past answers.
❖ Explain all of the steps or hurdles required in order to get the job

(The steps involved in selection are discussed in the next two chapters).

5

Screening -
Identifying Requirements,
The Prescreen and Testing

The second phase of the recruitment process is screening or selection. Screening involves trying to identify the best candidate or candidates. As with the other three phases, screening actually takes place from the initial contact all the way through the final close. That is, during, and even before, the initial contact the screening process is being conducted. For example, before engaging in a more formal contact with the candidate, many companies may want to determine whether a job candidate meets their minimum requirements, in other words conduct a form of prescreening during the precontact phase.

The primary function of screening is to identify the best people available for the job. However, the manner in which the best people are identified for the job will, in part, determine the perceptions you create of the company, the job, and of the type of person you are seeking for the position.

We are not proponents of the current view that the job candidate should be seen as a customer who must be served as quickly as possible, at least not when you are searching for hires for hard to fill positions. The job candidate is not a customer and anyone would have a right to be suspicious of a five minute selection process or a simple "when can you start?" message. Beyond the issue of the negative perceptions this may create in the minds of the job candidate, it simply does not allow enough time for effective screening.

Our primary purpose in this chapter, and the next, is to discuss the role of screening in recruiting the difficult hire and in creating a perceived climate of achievement. As a result, we do not deal in detail with the fine points of selection. Many excellent books exist which deal with selection as a topic in and of itself and several are listed in the references at the end of the book.

One technique used by many companies to screen candidates is to conduct a prescreen based upon the minimum qualifications for the position. While the actual process of establishing minimum qualifications will probably be carried out elsewhere in human resources, from our perspective minimum qualifications play an important role in creating perceptions and establishing standards.

Standardized tests can be used in many situations involving difficult hires, even when money is limited. Although a thorough understanding of testing and its role is beyond the scope of this book, it is important that the recruiter have a basic knowledge of testing.

Under the caps imposed by limited financial resources, it is quite logical that the selection interview serves as the major screening tool. We would argue that the type of selection interview which works best in screening is one which includes questions which tap behaviors. Given the importance of the selection interview in recruiting for the difficult hire, we have devoted a separate chapter, Chapter 6, to a discussion of the selection interview.

The properly designed screening process achieves the goals of control and changing perceptions. In addition, it leads to the gathering of critical information used to make decisions on the job candidate. Finally, the screening process is directly related to the establishment of standards and the fulfillment of individual needs. Through the establishment of high standards for selection into the job, we send a message to the job candidate that this is a quality company and a quality job. By meeting the high standards set for the job, the candidate meets their needs for achievement and affiliation.

Thus, while all of the basic principles apply, the following principles are particularly important in the screening process:

1. You must stay in control.

2. You must fulfill the individual's needs.

3. Set and keep your standards high.

How Do I Know What I Am Looking
for In a Candidate?

In a perfect world, the recruiter would be handed a complete job narrative which would provide all of the information necessary for conducting the screening process. This job narrative would be the result of analyses carried out by a trained professional and would be based upon extensive job analyses and validation studies. This job narrative would include:

❖ A job description, which is a complete listing of the job duties, tasks and responsibilities.

❖ A job specification, which is a listing of job requirements corresponding to the factors in a job evaluation system or compensation system.

❖ The minimum qualifications required by the job.

❖ The abilities required in order to perform the job.

Unfortunately, the world is far from perfect, and also constantly changing, and as a result the traditional notion of job analysis is currently being challenged as inflexible. In addition, in smaller companies, a complete job analysis may not be feasible due to the cost and time required.

As a supplement to job analysis, and sometimes a substitute for job analysis, we have developed a procedure based upon an analysis of the prototypical career paths of outstanding performers. Although describing the Prototypical Career Path method in detail is beyond the scope of this book, it is a useful technique to have in a recruiter's arsenal.

Basically, using the Prototypical Career Path method, the recruiter is interested in defining or identifying the personal requirements associated with successful job performance. That is, the Prototypical Career Path method allows the recruiter to answer the question "How do I know what I am looking for in a job candidate?" From a selection standpoint, the personal factors which need to be considered are:

❖ Past behaviors.

❖ Abilities — knowledge, skills, and aptitudes.

❖ Personality and needs.

Today, in human resource, we also see the term *competencies* used to refer to a combination or cluster of past behaviors, abilities, and personality. The steps in the Prototypical Career Path method include:

1. For a specific job, identify examples of high performers in the organization. For comparison purposes, it may also be worthwhile to identify poor or inadequate performers.

2. Schedule interviews with your high and low performers. Ask questions concerning the requirements of the job, but also find out what factors shaped their careers. How did they develop the abilities they now possess? What were significant milestones in their careers? What behavioral incidents helped to shape their career? If possible, obtain a copy of the high and low performers' resumes and determine how their career paths have differed.

3. Interview supervisors. Ask the supervisors similar questions to those in Step 2 above regarding high and low performers.

4. Based on the information obtained from the above, pre-pare a list of the required past behaviors, abilities, and person-ality factors which correlate with successful performance. In addition, map out the prototypical career path. What types of past experiences and career milestones appear to be related to successful performance; what would the job application or re-sume of a high performer look like?

The past behaviors, abilities, and personality factors associated with a job will tend to vary depending upon the nature of the occupation, the organization, and even the manager's supervisory style. However, we have found that there are certain generalities which can be identified regarding the prototypical career paths of successful performers at different levels in the organization.

Entry level jobs are those which typically involve a minimum requirement of only a high school degree and either very little or no previous experience. In scanning a job application or interviewing for jobs at the entry level, you should look for a pattern of stability and dependability. This may be demonstrated through either their previous school or work histories. Many times, the best performers come from those candidates whose work histories include stable employment in a job or industry where one must work hard, such as working for a moving company, a grocery store, or in a sales position with clear, hard goals. During the interview, attention should be paid to the manner in which a person dresses and to their basic communication skills. For office jobs, some minimum level of typing speed is often required and previous experience working with computers may be a real plus.

Professional jobs typically require a bachelor's degree, often in a specialized field such as accounting, finance, or human resource management. Individuals applying for jobs at this level may have very little previous experience which is directly relevant to the job. As a result, their academic achievements may be more relevant than their previous work experience. In scanning a resume and during the interview, you should look at the Grade Point Average (GPA), although what serves as a satisfactory GPA may vary by major and school. We have found that the best performers have academic histories which include involvement in outside activities and having taken leadership roles in student organizations.

Advanced Professional jobs typically require a bachelor's degree and two to three years of previous experience. In evaluating the quality of the previous experience, there should be evidence of steady career growth including promotions. At this point, the top performers have started to pay attention to their career potential and their own self-improvement. In response, the preferred job candidate will have joined professional organizations or sought out additional training opportunities. During the interview, you should attempt to assess interpersonal skills and potential supervisory and managerial ability.

At the Managerial-Executive level, jobs typically require a bachelor's degree and four to ten years of previous experience. In evaluating the quality of the previous experience, look for a steady pattern of promotions, at least one every two to three years, and a breadth or range of experiences. The individual may have been at more than one company, but should not be a job jumper. Typically, at this level, the top performers will have acquired additional education or training, including perhaps an MBA. During the interview, you should look for evidence of previous success in handling multiple roles and in leadership positions, both at work and in the community. By this point, the preferred candidate will have developed a clear personal mission statement and a well-defined view of the future.

The previous descriptions are provided as an example of how the Prototypical Career Path method works at a general level and are not intended to serve as a comprehensive list of qualifications for any position. In recruiting and hiring, you should also look for specialized abilities, especially abilities and personality traits which have been identified as job relevant.

Minimum Qualifications and the Prescreen

As the name suggests, the *minimum qualifications* are the minimum standards a candidate must meet to be considered for the job. Usually, minimum qualifications will be stated in terms of years of education and experience. For example, for a high profile secretarial position, the minimum requirements might be a high school degree plus five years of experience with word processing equipment. Do not be afraid to state the minimum requirements for a job early on, even in an advertisement or a job posting. If someone does not meet the minimum standards there is no reason for them to apply for the job. More importantly, the minimum qualifications communicate to the candidate that this job does have standards. If you do not state any minimum qualifications, it appears to the candidate that there are no standards for the job.

In the previous section, we discussed the use of the Prototypical Career Path method for establishing minimum qualifications. We would add the caution that minimum qualifications can become a major point of contention in attacking the validity of a selection system. As the name suggests, minimum qualifications should be set so as to correspond to a reasonable degree of competency as associated with minimally competent performers. While you want to establish a standard with your minimum qualifications, there should be a clear demonstration of job relatedness in setting minimum qualifications. This is especially true where the minimum qualifications may result in adverse impact (see Chapter 8), in which case we would recommend seeking professional guidance. Many organizations identify a set of qualifications for the preferred candidate in addition to any minimum qualifications.

In conducting the prescreen, an application or resume is usually compared to the minimum qualifications and other requirements of the job. As a recruiter, this may be your responsibility or it may be carried out elsewhere in human resources or management – or today may even be performed by a computer.

In reviewing the candidate's application and other information, as well as during the interview itself, you should watch for **Red Flags**. A red flag is a potential indicator that something is wrong. Some examples of red flags would be:

❖ The application is not completely filled out. The candidate forgot to fill out the back side or never even looked at the back side.

❖ There are conflicts between pieces of information. For example, a candidate indicates he received an MBA from a university in Florida at the same time he was employed in Wisconsin.

❖ There are prolonged periods of unemployment that are unexplained.

❖ The candidate has had a lot of jobs and only stayed at each for a short period of time.

❖ The candidate has an erratic career path with many different kinds of jobs.

❖ Functional resumes. In a functional resume, the person does not list jobs but instead lists the functions or tasks he has performed in the past. We know that a lot of career guidance counselors suggest the use of functional resumes and that one reason they are recommended for use is because they can hide a lot of holes and problems in someone's career history. However, this is also a good reason to be wary of functional resumes.

The presence of red flags does not necessarily mean that you should not interview the person. Nor does it mean that they may not turn out to be an excellent match for the job. You should, however, be sure to mark any red flags and develop questions to ask during the interview so as to cover each potential problem area.

The resume, or job application, can also be used to do a preliminary assessment of past behaviors and the possession of job related aptitudes, especially previous job knowledge. As indicated previously, the prescreen of the application or resume can also be used to compare the career history of the job candidate to the career paths of top performers in your organization. Any information gleaned from the prescreen should be used to develop follow-up questions for incorporation into the selection interview (see Chapter 6).

Tests

Standardized tests can play a major role in the selection process for hard to fill positions. Unfortunately, many companies resist testing or seem to think it is illegal, mysterious and perhaps even dangerous. Testing is seen as expensive and as something that is conducted by a clinical psychologist as a way of investigating the personality of an individual.

In psychology, a *test* is a structured sample or sign of behavior. Helping to confuse the matter, in human resources or from a legal perspective, a test could be considered to be anything used to make a selection or hiring decision including, but not limited to, the application form, the interview, reference checks and performance appraisals. We will take the narrower definition, where a test is defined as having structure in its:

❖ Content — similar questions, items or stimuli are administered to each test taker.

❖ Procedures — the test is taken under similar conditions by each person to whom the test is administered.

❖ Scoring — the test is scored in a similar manner for all test takers.

Tests can be judged based upon their reliability, validity, and utility. A test is reliable if similar scores are obtained when a test is administered repeatedly to the same test takers. Thus, reliability corresponds to what might be thought of as consistency. Frequently, reliability is actually assessed by determining whether the different internal parts of the test result in similar scores (technically, this is referred to as internal consistency reliability and is usually measured by obtaining an estimate of split-half reliability or coefficient alpha). Data on the reliability of tests should be available in the test manual or from the test's publisher.

Validity refers to whether the test is measuring the construct it is supposed to be measuring. More specifically, when used for employment or screening purposes, the validity of the test is defined based on the degree of relationship between the test and job performance and the accuracy of the inferences which can be made based upon the test regarding job performance. While the documentation of the validity of a test is a highly technical area, the methods used can be divided into content, criterion-related, and construct validity.

Utility involves an assessment as to whether the benefits from administering a test outweigh the costs associated with a test. Although some tests may be valid or reliable, it may not be practical to administer an expensive or time consuming instrument to large numbers of job candidates. The degree of adverse impact is another standard which is often used in evaluating the adequacy of a test. Adverse impact is discussed in Chapter 8.

For many people, their previous exposure to testing seems to be limited to classroom tests or limited knowledge of instruments such as the "Inkblot Test." There are, however, many types of tests which can be used for selection purposes, including:

- ❖ Job Knowledge
- ❖ Aptitude
- ❖ Work Sample
- ❖ Physical Ability
- ❖ Personality
- ❖ Assessment Centers
- ❖ Biographical Information Blanks (BIBs)

Job knowledge tests measure the specific areas of knowledge associated with the job. For example, a candidate for a paramedic position would be given a test measuring knowledge of first aid. A candidate for a real estate agent position might be given a test measuring knowledge of state laws regarding real estate transactions.

Aptitude tests measure a general competence or an ability to perform in a general domain. Some common aptitudes include general mental ability, verbal ability, mathematical ability, mechanical ability, and clerical aptitude. Examples of the use of aptitude tests would include administering a test of general mental ability to a candidate for a clerical position or administering a mechanical ability test to someone applying for a machine operator position.

Work sample tests require the candidate to actually perform the job, or parts of the job, under controlled conditions and are, thus, often used to measure skills, for example, a typing test to measure typing speed and accuracy. In some cases, the candidate may first be trained in how to perform the task; this is also called a trainability test. Examples of work sample tests would include asking a candidate for a mechanic's position to assemble an engine or asking a candidate for a sales position to engage in a simulated role play of a difficult encounter with a customer.

Physical ability tests assess physical agility and strength. Examples would include asking a candidate for police officer to run a mile or requiring a candidate for a moving company position to lift boxes weighing 75 pounds. The Americans with Disabilities Act of 1990 (ADA) may restrict the usage of physical ability tests for certain types of jobs. For more information on the ADA, see Chapter 8.

Personality tests measure aspects of the candidate's personality. Potential uses of a personality test would include administering a test to a candidate for a sales position to see if the person likes working with people – extroversion – or administering a test measuring reactions to stress to candidates for a customer service representative position. Examples of typical items from an objective personality test include:

❖ I would prefer a job which involves lots of paperwork.
- A. Strongly Disagree
- B. Disagree
- C. Neutral
- D. Agree
- E. Strongly Agree

❖ If you are not making enough money on your job, then you can always work more hours.
- A. Strongly Disagree
- B. Disagree
- C. Neutral
- D. Agree
- E. Strongly Agree

❖ I prefer challenging work.
- A. Strongly Disagree
- B. Disagree
- C. Neutral
- D. Agree
- E. Strongly Agree

Some personality tests, such as the *Thematic Apperception Test* or the *Rorschach Test,* incorporate much less structured stimuli and are referred to as projective tests.

Assessment centers are typically used with managerial and supervisory jobs. Technically, an assessment center is not so much a type of test as it is a method for administering and interpreting a battery of tests. Some of the tests or exercises used in an assessment center are role plays, leaderless group discussions, in-baskets (a type of managerial work sample), personality tests, and aptitude tests. Assessors are used in order both to evaluate performance on individual exercises and also for the purpose of combining the information into a final evaluation of the candidate.

BIBs are similar in concept to the old, weighted application form. Questions are asked regarding specific, past behaviors. Thus, an advantage of the BIB is that it collects data at the behavioral level. A disadvantage is that the scoring is complicated and somewhat difficult to understand. Some examples of items which might be found on a BIB include:

❖ How old were you when you first learned to drive a car?
    A. Under 16
    B. 16
    C. 16 - 20
    D. 21 or over

❖ How old were you when you got your first job?
    A. Under 16
    B. 16
    C. 16 - 20
    D. 21 or over

❖ What was your grade point average in college?
    A. Less than 2.00
    B. 2.00 - 3.00
    C. 3.00 - 3.50
    D. More than 3.50

Thus, there are many different types of tests which may be used for different types of jobs or situations. In screening for the position of Customer Service Representative, a representative test battery might include:

❖ A general aptitude tests which includes measures of verbal and mathematical ability.

❖ A measure of clerical speed and accuracy.

❖ A measure of the ability to follow written directions.

❖ A personality test which measures the Big Five and also provides a composite estimate of dependability and the likelihood of success in customer service positions.

❖ A typing test.

❖ A work sample test where the candidate is asked to respond to a phone call from a simulated customer.

Although testing can be expensive, it need not be. There are many test publishing companies which offer standardized tests at reasonable prices. Today, many tests can be administered and scored by computer, thereby alleviating much of the administrative burden. Your company may also want to consider having a test battery tailored to the job. While this is a more expensive option, when a company uses its own test battery rather than the same system everyone else in town is using to hire new employees, it sets the company apart as more prestigious and having higher standards.

In setting up a testing program, we would recommend consulting with an expert or a professional. Tests should be validated or shown to be job related – some basic testing references appear in Chapter 8. Validation may be conducted by an internal or external consultant or by a testing company.

While testing does involve some costs, research in Industrial-Organizational Psychology has shown that the benefits far outweigh the costs. Attributes of people which are very difficult or impossible to identify through the interview can be measured through testing. The bottom line is that testing leads to better hires than those who are selected when testing is not used.

From the perspective of recruiting for the difficult hire, testing plays an important role related to the basic principles. In particular, the use of tests allows the recruiter to:

1. Stay in control.

2. Fulfill the individual's needs.

3. Set and keep your standards high.

Testing is standardized which allows for the establishment of a climate of control. It says to the candidate you are going to do this and in the following order. More important, testing allows the recruiter and the company to demonstrate the commitment to high standards. It conveys to the candidate the message that the organization will not just accept anyone and that high standards exist for the job.

Thus, tests serve as a hurdle, a hurdle which indicates that the candidate has accomplished something worthwhile. By passing a test, the candidate fills their need for achievement. The candidate is also then in a position where they can brag to their friends and family that they passed a very difficult test battery. This allows the candidate to also meet their need for affiliation. If you place the candidate in a position where they can meet both their need for affiliation and their need for achievement, then basic psychology tells us they will have a favorable attitude toward you, the job, and the company. Some organizations prefer to contract out a portion of the recruitment function by working with employment or staffing agencies. If you do have to coordinate your human resource efforts with an outside agency, then you need to make sure that they are aware of the basic principles. Representatives of the agency should know as much as possible about your organization and your innovative approach to recruiting.

Summary

Screening involves trying to identify the best people for the job. In order to select the best people, you must collect job related information on the candidates. Hopefully your screening methods will not only identify the right people, but they will also attract the right people. Thus, screening also plays a recruiting role. The screening methods used serve as hurdles which provide the job candidate with a sense of accomplishment, achievement, and value. As a result, screening methods help to determine the perceptions you create of the company, the job, and of the type of person you are seeking for the position.

In the next chapter, we will discuss a third screening technique, the behavioral interview.

All seven basic principles apply to the screening process, but the following three basic principles are particularly critical:

1. You must stay in control.

2. You must fulfill the individual's needs.

3. Set and keep your standards high.

6

Screening – The Selection Interview

Traditionally, the selection interview was carried out in a person to person meeting. However, as the cost of face-to-face interviews in creases, many companies are moving to the use of phone interviews for screening purposes, or at least as part of the screening process. Therefore, the discussion in this chapter is applicable to both phone and in-person interviews.

Interviewing techniques are used during the:

1. Phone screen and initial interview.
2. Second interview with the recruiter.
3. Interview with appropriate supervisor or manager.

Of course, the exact nature of the interview will vary as a function of who is doing the interview and the type of job. Interviewing techniques may even be used during standardized testing.

As with tests, the selection interview is used to accomplish two goals. First, it should screen for the best people and the right people for the job. Second, it should shape and control perceptions, fulfill the individual's needs, and illustrate the high standards which exist for the job. In Chapter 4, we discussed at length the use of the interview as a control mechanism. In this chapter, we will concentrate on the use of the selection interview for screening purposes.

Although all of the basic principles are relevant to the selection interview, the following principles are particularly important:

1. Stay in control.
2. You must fulfill the individual's needs.
3. Set and keep your standards high.

Keys to the Successful Interview

In order to conduct a successful selection interview, the recruiter should:

❖ Prepare ahead of time.
❖ Watch for red flags.
❖ Watch for knock out factors.
❖ Assess factors which can only be evaluated during an interview.
❖ Use open-ended, behaviorally based questions in order to assess job related abilities.

The recruiter must prepare in advance for the interview. The basic agenda should be established ahead of time and a set of behaviorally based questions should already be prepared. The recruiter should have already reviewed the candidate's application, or resume, and any other information which might be available. For example, if other interviews have already been conducted or if tests have been administered, then the recruiter should be sure to review this information.

As an interviewer, you should be organized, be professional, and document what occurs during the interview. You need to make sure to take and maintain copious notes. The important rule to keep in mind during the interview is to write down everything (See Chapter 8).

Remember, when conducting the selection interview, you need to stay in control. Methods for staying in control were discussed in Chapter 4. In order to stay in control, you do not have to always be talking. Silence can be used to stay in control. Make use of silence by waiting a moderate amount of time after the candidate appears to finish before you respond. This will increase the chance the candidate will reveal important information.

Close attention should be paid to the candidate and to his choice of words. If the interview is conducted in person, use body language including nodding your head or leaning toward the candidate to encourage them to continue with their answer. If you find that certain words or topics elicit an emotional response, invite the candidate to elaborate on the topic. In addition, be sure to avoid questions which may be interpreted as being discriminatory against protected groups (see Chapter 8).

In a previous section on minimum qualifications, we mentioned the necessity of looking for red flags during the review of the candidate's application information, as well as during the interview itself. If you are not involved in the prescreen, then before the interview you need to perform a careful review of all of the available information on the candidate. In conducting this review, you should look for the presence of red flags, as they are a potential indicator that something is wrong. You should mark these red flags and develop questions to ask during the interview so as to cover each potential problem area.

For example, consider an applicant for the Customer Service Representative position whose resume indicates that she received a bachelor's degree in 1995, but then went back and received an associate's degree in music in 1999. The resume fails to note any work experience between 1995 and 1999. This raises several red flags. Why, after obtaining a bachelor's degree, did the job candidate go back to school for an associate's degree? Why did it take four years to receive what is typically a two-year degree? What else did the job candidate do during this time period? Why didn't the job candidate have a job during this time period? Perhaps the candidate has legitimate responses to each of these questions, or maybe the candidate has a spotty work history or has been unable to find other employment.

As the name suggests, "knock out factors" refer to information which has the effect of immediately disqualifying a candidate from consideration for the job. Often times, knock outs responses occur in response to a related question, since the recruiter would never think of asking a direct question on the topic. Some examples we have encountered of knock outs include:

❖ In interviewing a police officer candidate, the interviewer asks "What would you do if someone was running away from you and an officer ordered you to shoot the suspect." Reply from candidate, "Oh, I could never shoot or kill anyone. I do not believe in violence."

❖ In interviewing a firefighter, the interviewer asks "What would you do if you were at the top of an aerial ladder and a high wind came up." Reply from candidate, "I wouldn't go up the ladder in the first place. I am afraid of heights."

❖ In interviewing a candidate for a commission-based, salesperson position, the interviewer asks, "Tell me about a time in the past where you have had to work on commission and how you responded?" Reply from the candidate, "I would not work on commission. I will only work if I am paid a regular salary."

There are some factors which are very difficult to assess outside of the interview. Therefore, the recruiter should pay special attention to the evaluation of behaviors related to:

❖ Appearance
❖ Oral communication skills
❖ Resistence to stress
❖ Future career goals

In conducting the interview, the recruiter needs to beware of falling into the trap of asking closed-ended questions. Avoid questions which can be answered with a simple yes or no. If you do ask such a question, follow it up with open-ended questions.

Open-ended questions get the applicant to talk. For example, consider the case of Chris applying for the position of Customer Service Representative at First Rollins Bank. You have decided to ask about Chris's previous retail sales experience. A question you would want to avoid is:

"Did you ever work in retail sales?"

This question can be answered with a simple yes or no. A better way to phrase the question would be:

"Chris, tell me about a job you have had working in retail sales?"

If the candidate responds to an open-ended question with a minimal answer, then you need to follow up. You also should follow up if you do not receive all of the information you need. In response to each question, you need to be sure to get the following information:

❖ Where – Where did this take place? What company? During what time period?

❖ Who – Who were the other people involved? What roles did they play in the situation?

❖ What – What was the exact situation involved? What did the candidate do? What actions did the candidate take?

❖ Why – Why was it that the candidate took the actions she did?

❖ Payoff – What were the results? What were the outcomes?

One way to remember the above is W4P. That is, you should always get information on Where, Who, What, Why, and the Payoff.

The question above about working in retail sales is often referred to as a behaviorally based question. A significant portion of the selection interview should always be devoted to asking these behaviorally based questions. The interview format which incorporates behaviorally based questions is sometimes referred to as a structured interview, because by asking behaviorally based questions the recruiter keeps the interview structured and under control.

An important psychological principle is that past performance (or behavior) is the best predictor of future performance (or behavior). If an applicant for a sales job met all of their quotas on the last sales job, then the odds are good that they will meet whatever quotas exist on a future sales job. Certainly, situations do influence behavior and just because someone did something in the past, does not necessarily mean they will or can repeat it. However, in hiring we must go with averages or probabilities, and the probability is that past behavior is a good indicator of future behavior. Specific questions about how an applicant handled a past situation allow us to gain insight into how they will handle future situations and allow us to predict their future behavior in similar situations.

The basis of behaviorally based interviewing is that by asking questions about past behavior, predictions can be made concerning future behavior. It should be noted, however, that behaviorally based interviewing need not be limited to just past behavior, the recruiter might want to ask questions about predicted behavior or future behavior.

Sometimes, asking questions about future behavior is a necessity. For example, in hiring firefighters or police officers, most of the candidates may not have previously performed a similar job or task. So, we might ask a police officer what they would do if they had to shoot someone. Similarly, if we are hiring high school students, they may have limited previous work experience. Therefore, we might phrase some of our questions so as to reflect what someone might do or might not do in a particular situation. The important element is not the time aspect, but whether the questions are behaviorally based and can be answered in terms of specific behaviors. An interview format which is structured and incorporates questions concerning what a candidate would do in a simulated situation is sometimes referred to as a situational interview.

Here are some examples of behaviorally based questions for the candidate, Chris Spears, who is applying for the Customer Service Representative position and has claimed to have previous job experience with Big Met Telephone Company as a customer service representative. The first four questions deal with past behaviors. The next four questions deal with how the candidate would respond in a future situation.

❖ *"Chris, when you were customer service rep for Big Met, how did you handle the most difficult customer with whom you ever dealt? Tell me about it."*

❖ *"Think about the last difference of opinion you had with a co-worker, what did you do to resolve it?"*

❖ *"Tell me what steps you took at Big Met to increase your likelihood of being promoted."*

❖ *"Tell me about a time at Big Met where you had to be particularly creative or innovative in order to solve a problem?"*

❖ *"Chris, if you come to work here at First Rollins Bank, you might be asked to train new associates when they are hired. Imagine a situation where your supervisor has asked you to volunteer to train new associates, how would you respond?"*

❖ *"Imagine a situation where you and your supervisor have just had a big disagreement. How would you handle this situation?"*

❖ *"You are on your way to work when your car breaks down. You know that you are going to be late for work. What would you do?"*

❖ *"You are talking on the phone to a customer, and he starts to yell and swear at you. How would you handle this situation?"*

Of course, the content of the questions would vary as a function of the type of job, the results of the Prototypical Career Path analysis, and the ability and personality requirements.

Scoring

The selection interview must result in some type of pass-fail decision. However, there are a number of methods which can be used to reach this final decision. The simplest procedure is for the interviewer to arrive at a pass-fail judgment. If this method is used, it should be accompanied by documentation reflecting the rationale behind the final rating. Other holistic methods include using a rating scale with additional steps, such as "fail-marginal pass-pass," a 1 to 5 scale, or a 1 to 10 scale. Another holistic alternative is to rank the candidates based upon their interview results. However, at some point the user of any of these other systems must still reach a final decision as to whether the candidate has passed the hurdle and may move on to the next step.

It is also possible to rate each response to a question separately and then sum the scores in the same manner as would be done with a test. Examples of questions and potential rating scales for the obtained responses follow:

❖ Question: "You are working selling women's clothing and are paid a commission. Your supervisor asks you to take some time to straighten up the store. What would you do?"

5 Would straighten the floor and do the best job possible including keeping an eye out for prospective customers. Indicates knowing that a store with a neat appearance helps to attract customers and that means more sales.

3 Would straighten the floor only if forced to do so by the supervisor. Would do enough to get by and keep the supervisor happy.

1 Would refuse to do it. Would get mad and also refuse to wait on customers.

❖ Question: "Tell me about a time where a supervisor wanted you to work overtime?"

5 Told the supervisor that they were happy to work the overtime. Saw working overtime as a chance to get ahead and as an opportunity to demonstrate devotion to the company and customer service.

3 Worked the overtime, however, was not happy about it and let the supervisor know that they were unhappy.

1 Refused to work the overtime. Left without saying anything. Pretended they were never asked.

Another general method of scoring is to produce ratings of behavioral categories, competencies, or abilities based upon all of the information collected during the interview. Thus, the recruiter provides ratings for summary scales rather than for individual questions. In making the ratings, the interviewer considers the match between the behaviors exhibited or described during the interview and the behavioral anchors of the rating scales. Examples for several different constructs appear below:

❖ Oral Communication

5 Very easy to understand and comprehend. Speech was fluid. Thoughts were well organized and presented clearly. Spoke at a proper rate and a proper volume. Made sure that the listener understood what was being said.

3 Presented information, but in a manner which was difficult to follow at times. Flow of ideas was choppy. On occasion, voice was too soft or too loud.

1 Difficult to understand. Frequently lost track of thoughts or wandered onto inappropriate topics. Voice was frequently too soft or too loud.

❖ Motivation for Customer Service

5 Does what it takes, and then more, in order to get the job done. Takes initiative and puts in extra effort when needed. Attempts to identify and solve problems and takes responsibility when things go wrong. Wants respect. Has a strong need for achievement.

3 Does only what is required. Will work overtime, but only if required to do so. Solves problems only after the issue has been pointed out to them. Works just hard enough to get the job done.

1 Is not concerned with the quantity or the quality of work. Does not care what supervisors or coworkers think. Very reluctant to do extra work or work overtime. Takes no pride in the quality of the work performed.

❖ Development of Others

5 Brings out the best in others. Can deal with people issues, performance issues, and ideas. Challenges others to perform. Sets challenging goals for others. Coaches others. Provides feedback to others.

3 Does what it takes to get the job done, however, has trouble delegating responsibilities. Sets general goals for groups and individuals rather than specific goals. Has trouble giving feedback. Tends to choose one leadership style and stick with it regardless of the situation. Has trouble giving negative feedback to subordinates.

1 Has difficulty working with others. Makes promises which cannot be kept. Gives inaccurate feedback. Creates a negative atmosphere. Does not set goals. Does not recognize the contributions of others.

Of course, with the rating scale methods, some procedure must be adopted for arriving at a cutting score corresponding to a pass-fail decision. This cutting score could be established for the overall total score or for ratings on individual scales.

Remember it is through setting the high standards on each of the five hurdles that the appropriate climate of achievement is created. By passing each hurdle, the job candidate fulfills his or her needs for achievement and affiliation. With each hurdle successfully completed, the candidate should be congratulated on the accomplishments.

Avoiding Rating Errors

In scoring or rating the interview, you need to learn to identify and avoid common rater errors. How can an interviewer avoid rating errors? Research suggests that the common rating errors can be reduced through relatively short training programs. Some of the more common errors include:

❖ Scale usage errors
❖ The similar to me effect
❖ Contrast effects
❖ Halo error

Scale usage errors refer to a rater's tendency to use only one part of the rating scale regardless of the true score (the score a job candidate would receive if their performance was rated by a perfectly accurate interviewer; of course, this true rating can never really be known). Leniency occurs when a rater tends to give all the job candidates a high rating on all of the questions or dimensions (4 or 5 on a 1 to 5 scale), regardless of the true score. Central tendency occurs when the rater tends to give all the job candidates an average rating on all of the dimensions (3 on a 1 to 5 scale), regardless of the true score. Strictness occurs when a rater tends to give all the job candidates a low rating on all the dimensions (1 on a 1 to 5 scale), regardless of the true score. In order to avoid scale usage errors, make sure that you use all the points of the scale when appropriate. Contrary to popular belief, everyone is not above average.

The similar to me effect occurs when the recruiter and the candidate have a lot in common. When there is a great deal of similarity between the recruiter and the job candidate, there is a tendency for the rater to think that "If I am a good worker, then this candidate will be a good worker also, since we have so much in common." Of course, just because a candidate went to the same school you attended does not mean that he will be an equally valued employee. In order to avoid the similar to me effect, stick with the structured interview and record all of the responses, even if the candidate could be your twin. When your interview notes are reviewed at a later time, you may find that you have overlooked some of the job candidate's less positive attributes.

Contrast effects occur when the evaluation of one candidate is influenced by the evaluation of another candidate. Consider the case of an interview with an average job candidate (one who would be a 3 on a 1 to 5 scale). If that candidate is interviewed right after you have met with the world's worst recruit, then, in all likelihood, your tendency will be to rate the average candidate as above average. On the other hand, if the average candidate is interviewed right after you have met with the perfect recruit, then, in all likelihood, your tendency will be to rate the average candidate as below average. In order to avoid contrast effects, you should make sure that you are comparing candidates to the standards and not to each other.

Halo error occurs when you develop a general impression of a candidate and then allow that general impression to affect your rating of all of the behaviors, questions or dimensions (this assumes you are providing ratings of individual dimensions in addition to an overall rating). A related error is the first impression error, which occurs when we make a quick judgment regarding a person and allow this initial impression to color the processing of later information. However, even a very strong candidate can have weaknesses. A candidate for a Customer Service Representative position may score above average on every dimension except resistence to stress (and, may still be an acceptable employee even if they have one area of weakness). In order to avoid halo error, consider the behavioral evidence for each dimension independently.

As we indicated previously, knowledge is one of the best defenses against rating errors. In addition, rating errors can be avoided by using a structured, selection interview and by evaluating the candidate based upon only job related information. Providing accurate ratings is but one more example of the need for the recruiter to stay in control of his or her own attitudes and perceptions during the recruitment process.

Summary

Screening involves trying to identify the best people for the job. Besides screening, the selection interview also plays an important role in creating and controlling perceptions. By including behaviorally based questions in the selection interview, the recruiter is able to increase structure and control while at the same time sending the message to candidates that this is a job which must be earned. The result is that the selection interview serves as a hurdle which provides the job candidate with a sense of accomplishment and achievement while also creating a climate of achievement.

In order to conduct a successful selection interview, the recruiter should:

❖ Prepare ahead of time.
❖ Watch for red flags.
❖ Watch for knock out factors.
❖ Assess factors which can only be evaluated during an interview.
❖ Use open-ended, behaviorally based questions in order to
  assess job related abilities.
❖ Evaluate or score the results in an unbiased fashion.

All seven basic principles apply to the selection interview, but the following three basic principles are particularly critical:

1. You must stay in control.
2. You must fulfill the individual's needs.
3. Set and keep your standards high.

7

Closing — Selling the Job

As mentioned previously, we are not proponents of the currently popular philosophy that the job candidate should be viewed as a customer, nor of the view that recruiting is another type of marketing. At some point, however, the recruiter must bring the recruitment process to some type of final resolution. Thus, recruiting and sales do have the close in common. The recruiter must try to convince the candidate to continue with the recruitment process until the point is reached at which the candidate must make a final decision as to whether to accept or reject the job. The process of convincing the candidate to commit to the next step, whether it is another interview or taking the job, we refer to as the close.

All of the basic principles apply to the close. Hopefully, by the time the candidate gets to the final close, the decision as to whether to accept a job offer, you have firmly established each of the seven basic principles. If you have, then the odds are good that with the proper close the candidate will accept the job offer. In addition, the following four principles are particularly important during the close:

1. You must stay in control.
2. Control the negatives.
3. You must fulfill the individual's needs.
4. Set and keep your standards high.

Emphasize the High Standards

During any meetings or conversations with the candidate, be sure to mention the five hurdles repeatedly and emphasize the high standards in place

72

for the selection of new hires. If you are asked what the company is looking for in new hires, then simply mention the qualities you are looking for and the existence of the multiple hurdles or screens.

As the candidate completes each step, be sure to offer appropriate congratulations. Let the candidate know how hard it is to get through each step and let them know that they have really accomplished something. Watch the reaction of the candidate as you acknowledge their successful completion of another step. If they seem pleased with you and with themselves, then you have identified a promising candidate for the position.

At this point you may want to review the discussion from Chapter 3 on the Psychology of the Job Candidate. A job candidate will be unmotivated to take a position if it is apparent that anyone could get the job! For example, please consider which would you rather be told:

A *"We would hire anyone who walked through the door for this job. Are you breathing? You are hired."*

Or,

B *"Our company is a quality company. We only believe in hiring the best. That is why we have put you through a rigorous screening process. As a result of our highly selective process, we have determined that you are one of the best. We would like to offer you a position."*

No doubt, your choice was B. B conveys a sense that something important has been accomplished and that achievement has taken place.

If you find what you think is a great candidate, you may find yourself wanting to respond to the question of *"how soon are you hiring?"* with a *"Today! Do you want to start this Monday?"* But, don't! Beyond the danger of being misled by a first impression and hiring the wrong person, you need and want to come across as selective. More important, the job candidate also wants you to come across as selective. So, a better response to the above question would be:

"Chris, our selection process involves five steps which include:

1. A prescreen, which you have already passed.
2. An initial interview by phone.
3. Standardized tests.
4. An interview with the Human Resource Director.
5. An interview with the Manager.

We hire or make our offer as soon as the individual has successfully passed all five of these screening devices."

The existence of these five steps should be discussed and emphasized throughout the recruitment process. As a candidate completes each step, they should be congratulated, but also reminded of the remaining steps. It is through the steps that the recruiter instills a climate of achievement.

By setting up and clearly establishing the existence of steps, you create the perception that the job is something to be valued while also controlling the process. In addition, you provide the candidate with the opportunity to experience a real sense of accomplishment if the position is offered to them. You create a climate for achievement. So, do not be afraid to repeat the existence of the steps or hurdles. Based upon our experience, it is much more likely that a recruiter will under emphasize rather than over emphasize the five hurdles.

Closing the Initial Contact

The mechanism used to close the initial contact, and any follow up interview or testing sessions, is the **alternate choice close**. An alternate choice close is one in which the recruiter controls the options available to the candidate. That is, the recruiter suggests specific alternatives in terms of times and dates for the next meeting.

For example, during the initial contact you decide to invite this candidate for an in-person interview. When setting up this interview, avoid open-ended questions such as, *"When do you want to come in for an interview?"* This may convey any of several messages to the candidate, all of which are negative. Some of the many negative messages which may be conveyed to the candidate are:

❖ You are hard up and are desperate to hire someone.
❖ You will see the candidate whenever it is convenient for them.
❖ You have lots of time on your hands.
❖ You do not really care.

Note that in terms of the basic principles, you have handed control over to the candidate. You have lost control, and you have created the potential for negative perceptions.

The following would be an example of the use of the alternate choice close. Instead of leaving an opening for the candidate, you state:

> *"Chris, let me check my schedule to see what I have open . . . I have an opening at 10:00 tomorrow morning or 4:30 in the afternoon tomorrow. Which do you prefer?"*

After the candidate chooses one of the alternatives, you would then give directions to the interview site. Giving directions is another foot in the door which signals seriousness on both your part and the candidate's. You would then confirm the agreement as follows:

> *"Great, Chris, I'll see you at 10:00 tomorrow morning, here at my office at First Rollins Bank."*

You will want to repeat this statement several times as part of your closing comments in order to ensure commitment and to make sure that it is firmly imprinted in the candidate's mind. Another technique is to tell the candidate to get a pen and piece of paper and write it down. This accomplishes two important objectives. First, it is another sign of commitment on the candidate's part. Second, many candidates become both nervous and excited regarding the possibility of a job interview. They hang up the phone and turn to a family member and say *"You won't believe it. I have an interview at First Rollins Bank tomorrow. Oh no, I got so excited, I forgot the time and place."* So, help the candidate out, provide multiple reminders of the time and place of the next session, and be sure that the candidate puts the information down in writing. The last few words to the candidate should include mention of the time and place.

In corresponding with the candidate, you need to make sure that they know your name, your position title, and how you can be reached. Repeat your name throughout any contacts and make sure that they use your name when addressing you. By using the candidate's names and forcing the candidate to use your name, you initiate a personal relationship.

At the end of the conversation, you should repeat everything again. Two basic psychological principles related to memory are that:

1. Individuals have troubling storing more than seven pieces of information in short-term memory.

2. Recall is better for material presented at the beginning or the end of the conversation than it is for information which is presented during the middle of a conversation.

Therefore, in closing a conversation with a job candidate, the recruiter should be sure to summarize all of the important facts — who, where and when. An example is as follows:

> *"Wonderful, Chris. I am looking forward to seeing you. I'll see you at 10:00 tomorrow morning, here at my office. My name again is Pat Davis, at First Rollins Bank. That is 10:00 tomorrow. Good Bye."*

Do not be afraid to repeat yourself; do not worry about redundancy. Our recommendation is that you repeat all important facts at least five times during the conversation. Be sure to wrap up the conversation by mentioning the time again.

Closing the Testing Session and Other Interviews

The process of closing the various steps of the selection process is similar to the close for the initial contact. The alternate choice close should be used to establish future interview or testing dates and times. The candidate should be congratulated on the accomplishments to this point and informed of the hurdles still to come. Remember, there is value in repetition. By repeating the steps, you help to create a climate of achievement.

Not the Right Person

What happens if a person fails one of the hurdles or does not appear to be the best person for the job? The answer depends upon both where you are in the recruitment process and how close a relationship you have developed with the job candidate. If it is early in the process and there is not much rapport built up with the candidate, then it should be sufficient to send a simple postcard or letter. If it is later in the process, then it would be better to make a telephone call or send a personal letter. A personal call could also be used for the purpose of tying up any loose ends which may exist, such as reimbursements for travel expenses or mileage.

The Final Close

At this point, we will assume that the candidate has passed all of the hurdles or steps and the decision has been made to make the person an offer. We will refer to the process of presenting the candidate with the offer as the *final close*. We will also assume for purposes of our discussion here that the recruiter is not in the position to negotiate features of the job such as pay, as consideration of this topic would take us beyond the bounds of the current book.

By the time the candidate gets to the final close, hopefully the recruiter has already established each of the seven basic principles and has congratulated the candidate on completing each of the steps. The candidate has been made to sweat a little and work hard for the opportunity to be offered the position. If a climate of achievement has been created, then the odds are good that with the proper close the candidate will not only accept the job offer but will also feel that they have really earned the job. They will be proud of themselves and have a positive image of you and the company. The candidate will be eager to tell their friends and family about the experience and about their new job. They will want the job — they will be waiting nervously, hoping you are going to offer them the job.

As with all the different processes involved in hiring, you will want to be consistent in your approach to making job offers and also documenting the results or responses to your job offers. It is quite common to make the initial offer verbally and then to follow up in writing.

As with the previous steps, we recommend that you use the alternate choice close. Present a series of options to choose from rather than asking an open-ended question. Avoid statements such as:

❖ *"Do you want the job?"*

❖ *"I hope after all this you take the job. We really need someone. My boss said he would fire me if I did not hire someone today."*

❖ *"When do you want to start?"*

Using the alternate choice close, the recruiter would say:

"Chris, I have really good news for you. You have achieved a lot. You have gone through five very difficult steps. Your test scores were good. I talked with the bank managers and they were very impressed. Chris, we are offering you the position of Customer Service Representative. Your pay rate will be $10 an hour and the benefits and incentive pay will be as we discussed before. We have

a new training class starting on the 1ˢᵗ of the month and on the 15ᵗʰ of the month. Chris, which of the training dates do you prefer?"

After the candidate chooses, you would then confirm your agreement as follows:

"Great, Chris, I will be sending you a letter which contains the details of our offer in writing. I'll see you at 8:00 on the 1ˢᵗ here at my office at First Rollins Bank. Congratulations on your new position. Chris, I look forward to working with you."

You will want to repeat this statement several times in order to ensure commitment and to make sure that it is firmly imprinted in the overly excited candidate's mind. Again, have the new employee write it down. At the end of the conversation, you should take the time to repeat everything again.

Of course, there may be negatives. As indicated previously, if the salary for the job is low or the working conditions are poor, then you need to emphasize the positive sides of the job offer package. Find the positive aspects of the total job package and emphasize these positive aspects, this may include emphasizing total compensation or alternative salary arrangements.

The candidate may also indicate a desire to wait to make a decision, perhaps even indicating that they are considering other offers. Again, the key is to maintain control and stick with the alternate choice close.

For entry level or lower level jobs, such as the Customer Service Representative at First Rollins Bank, a simple statement would be:

"Well, Chris, our training classes are filling up. As I said, we have a new training class starting on the 1ˢᵗ of the month and on the 15ᵗʰ of the month. We really need a decision from you now as to which you would prefer?"

While forcing the candidate to make an immediate decision may seem a bit extreme, please remember that the basis of our philosophy is that by this point the candidate desperately wants to receive an offer from the company. Hopefully, at this point, from the candidate's point of view, the question is not one of whether they will accept an offer, but rather a question of whether you will make them an offer. If you, as a recruiter, have followed the principles and created the right climate, then the job candidate should be ready to accept the job.

The research literature is somewhat divided on this point. Some studies indicate that candidates are just waiting for one offer, any offer, and tend to take the first offer they receive. On the other hand, other research suggests that candidates prefer to have some time to decide and prefer to have at least two offers before making a decision. Our opinion is that with difficult hires the recruiter must control the situation, and the best way to ensure control is through the use of the alternate choice close.

On occasion, it is reasonable to expect that a candidate might indicate they need to go home and discuss the offer with their family. Although we recommend trying to obtain an immediate decision, we have no problem in our own work with giving a candidate a day or a weekend to discuss the new opportunity with their family. In that case, an alternate close might take the form of saying to the candidate:

> *"Well, Chris, I understand your need to discuss this offer with your family. I am quite sure that they will be proud of you for receiving this offer. Why don't you take the weekend and talk it over with your family? As I said though, we do have new training classes starting on the 1st of the month and on the 15th of the month and I really need a decision as to which you would prefer? Chris, I will tell you what, take the weekend to discuss this with your family, and then call me before 9:00 A.M. on Monday. At that time, you can let me know whether you prefer the training class starting on the 1st or the 15th."*

With higher level jobs, not only do we recommend trying for an immediate reply from the candidate, we believe it should be even easier for the job candidate to provide you with a rapid response to a job offer. In the case of recruiting for the higher level job, you have probably already invested a lot of your time and money, and the company's time and money, in the search. The job candidate has probably been interviewed by high ranking managers and executives. At this point in the process, you should know which job candidate is your number one selection, and you should have a good idea as to whether your company is the job candidate's number one pick. Hopefully, the company's number one pick is also the person who really wants a job with your company.

If you find that your company is the second or third choice of the desired job candidate, then you need to negotiate with the candidate and try to discover why your company is not number one. Does the candidate have certain misconceptions concerning your company? Can you change those perceptions? If the candidate sees you as a friendly liaison within the company, then offer to sit down with the individual and compare the features of the competing offers in order to determine what is really best for the person. In doing so, you should try to identify what the job candidate sees as the important characteristics in making a job decision, and emphasize what your company has to offer in terms of those factors. Ask yourself what are the candidate's needs, and how can I show the candidate that my company best meets those needs.

If your company is not even being given serious consideration by a job candidate to whom you have made an offer, then it is quite possible that you have done something wrong in the recruitment process. You need to ask yourself what is was that you should have known or been able to spot earlier which would have indicated to you that there was a mismatch between the candidate and the company. For example, if a candidate's resume indicated that they were making $120,000, and you brought them in to interview for a job which pays $80,000, then you should not be too surprised if in rejecting the offer they tell you they just wanted some experience applying for jobs and were using you to try to get a better offer from another company. At this point, you may be tempted to blame your company for not offering enough money. However, it is more likely that you made the error by not screening out candidates whose salary demands were obviously outside the range which the company could hope to offer to a new hire. One potential negative consequence is that you may have missed the candidate you should have targeted initially. A second danger is that you may start to lose the confidence of executives and upper level managers in your own company. Nevertheless, you should learn from your failures. Try to identify what is was that you did wrong and work on correcting that mistake in the future.

Research has found that the factors which lead to the *acceptance* of a job offer may be different from the factors which lead to the *rejection* of a job offer. More specifically, location is not usually listed as one of the more important reasons for accepting a job, but is a major factor in rejecting job offers. If the location of the company, in terms of geographical area, is a problem, then you should be prepared to change that perception.

Summary

The close refers to the process of convincing the candidate to commit to the next step, whether the next step is taking a test, agreeing to another interview or taking the job (the final close). While all of the basic principles apply to the close, the following four principles are particularly important:

1. You must stay in control.
2. Control the negatives.
3. You must fulfill the individual's needs.
4. Set and keep your standards high.

In closing the initial contact, and any follow up interview or testing session, the recruiter should use the *alternate choice close*. An alternate choice close is one in which the recruiter controls the options available to the candidate by offering a limited number of alternatives from which the candidate can choose.

By the time the candidate reaches the point where they must accept or reject the job offer, the climate of achievement should have been established to the point where the candidate feels as if they have earned the job and the job is theirs. If the recruiter has firmly established each of the seven basic principles, then the candidate should be ready to accept the job.

8

Ensuring Equal
Employment Opportunity

In order to effectively recruit, screen, and select for hard to fill positions, one must have a familiarity with and knowledge of relevant court cases, legal principles and professional guidelines. The amount of information you need to know regarding these topics will depend upon your level within the organization and the functions you perform as a part of the recruitment process. Obviously, the Human Resource Director must be more knowledgeable than a supervisor who is involved only occasionally in the recruitment process.

Regardless of a person's level in the organization, everyone should have some knowledge of the laws and guidelines relevant to the functions being performed. For organizations receiving money from the United States Government, Office of Federal Contract Compliance Programs (OFCCP) guidelines require that personnel involved in hiring be familiar with the company's affirmative action plan.

In this chapter, our intent is to provide a basic overview of laws, guidelines and professional principles which those involved in recruitment should find useful. We have found it necessary to limit ourselves to the United States, as those are the laws the authors encounter on a regular basis. Many countries do have civil rights legislation similar to that which exists in the United States and we would encourage readers in other countries to become familiar with the applicable laws in their county.

As a caveat to the reader, the authors of this book are not lawyers. The comments presented here are not intended to substitute for legal advice. There are many excellent employment or human resource lawyers, and we would highly recommend contacting qualified legal professionals if questions arise regarding the propriety of the hiring process.

Many laws and regulations which apply to recruiting and hiring vary by state, and certainly vary by country. Within the United States, individual states often have their own idiosyncratic guidelines or laws on what questions may be asked during the interview. Benefit issues, such as unemployment compensation and workman's compensation, are often controlled by state laws which vary dramatically from state to state. We would recommend that recruiters, especially those who are involved in making human resource decisions, consider attending a legal workshop covering the laws applicable to their state.

We begin the chapter by discussing two basic principles:

1. Document, Document, Document — make sure all procedures, processes and decisions are documented.

2. Consistency — apply your procedures in a consistent manner for all job candidates.

We then consider the need to differentiate between the term *job candidate* and the term *applicant*. This is followed by a discussion of the difference between the disparate treatment and disparate impact definitions of discrimination. The remainder of the chapter is then devoted to a presentation of laws and professional guidelines applicable to equal employment and affirmative action efforts.

Document, Document, Document

One simple suggestion is that all procedures and decisions should be well documented. Any interview procedures used should be described in appropriate detail, including the existence of any standardized questions and scoring systems developed for use in the behavioral interview. Testing procedures should be standardized and described in detail, and records should be maintained on the results of testing sessions. The reasons for decisions, including those made by both the recruiter and the job candidate, should be noted and recorded. If someone is rejected for a job, document the reasons for the denial. If someone turns down your job offer, document their decision and the rationale behind their refusal. If in doubt - document.

Consistency

The second simple suggestion is consistency. If you have rules or procedures, apply them in a similar fashion to all candidates. Even if your top performing manager wants to hire a specific person, that job candidate must go through the same hiring process as everyone else. If the president of the company wants to hire a relative, that individual must go through the same hiring process as everyone else. The exception would be when reasonable accommodations are needed for some reason, such as the presence of a disability. If exceptions are made, be sure to document the reasons for the exceptions (although recent court cases suggest that companies need to be careful in identifying scores from tests taken under special circumstances such as accommodating a disability).

Defining Applicants

In the beginning of this book, we made the conscious choice to avoid the use of the term applicant and to use instead the term job candidate. This decision was made because the term applicant carries with it many additional meanings and the manner in which companies define applicants can have far reaching implications.

An applicant should be defined by the company and not by default. Just because someone sends in a resume, it does not mean that they should be considered an applicant. However, the procedure for defining applicants must then be established and documented. Companies need to be very careful in defining applicants. The definition of applicants should be a matter which is given careful thought, involves the company's attorneys, and is well documented.

One approach is to distinguish between applicants and qualified applicants. A job candidate, someone who has expressed an interest in the company in some manner, becomes an applicant when the company officially identifies them as someone whose application or resume will be reviewed for a specific job or opening with the company. A job candidate becomes a qualified applicant when it has been determined that their background meets the minimum requirements for the job.

> **Example:** On June 1st, an application from Chris Spears for the position of Customer Service Representative is received in the Human Resources office at First Rollins Bank. At this point, Chris is not yet officially an applicant. On June 7th, Pat Davis begins to process the applications which are currently on file as having been received for Customer Service Representative. All the applications, including the one from Chris Spears, which contain the necessary information and indicate a desire to obtain the position of Customer Service Representatives are sorted into one pile and are officially identified as applicants. Chris is now officially an applicant. The rest of the applications, those which do not contain sufficient information or appear to be for some other job, are discarded or filed. Pat returns to the stack of applications which met the first screen, and are now considered to be applicants, and compares the information on those applications to the minimum qualifications and other requirements of the job. If the information suggests that the applicant meets or exceeds the minimum requirements and other standards, they are now identified as a qualified applicant and scheduled for an initial contact. Chris is now a officially a qualified applicant.

For public sector companies, the definition of applicant is often made much easier due to civil service requirements. Jobs are posted, remain open for a certain period, and applications are accepted. If the application is received within the appropriate time period, completed in a timely manner, and meets certain standards, then the job candidate is considered an applicant. The applicant's background is then compared against the minimum qualifications. If the candidate meets or exceeds the standards, then they are considered to be a qualified applicant. While this procedure is very formal and can be restrictive at times, many private sector companies would be well served by developing more formal procedures for distinguishing between job candidates, applicants and qualified applicants.

This problem of differentiating between applicants and job candidates has become even more critical in the current era of Internet recruiting. Companies may receive resumes from job candidates who have no concept of what jobs they are even applying for with the organization. Candidates may apply repeatedly for the same job, sending their resume in day after day or several times within the same online session. Organizations need to establish policies for determining how to deal with resumes received over the Internet so that they can arrive at an accurate calculation of qualified applicants.

Disparate Treatment and Disparate Impact

There are two broad theories of discrimination – disparate treatment and disparate impact. Basically, disparate treatment is intentional discrimination and involves differences in decision making based on a person's protected status. For example, if only African-American job candidates were required to take a personality test, this could be construed as discrimination under a disparate treatment theory. While the previous example would rely upon rather direct evidence of discrimination, it is possible to establish disparate treatment based upon only circumstantial evidence — such as statistical evidence which suggests a pattern of clear discrimination. It is also possible to combine direct evidence with statistical evidence in putting forward an argument that disparate treatment has occurred.

During an interview, disparate treatment could be present if different questions are asked of job candidates as a function of their race, sex, or some other protected characteristic. That is why consistency is so important; disparate treatment can be avoided by asking the same questions of every candidate. A major benefit of the structured, behaviorally based interview is that all candidates for a position have the opportunity to respond to the same set of questions.

An exception to the prohibition on selection based upon a protected characteristic is where a Bona Fide Occupational Qualifications (BFOQ) exists. True and defensible BFOQs are very rare. It is unlikely that a BFOQ would be reasonable for the typical office job. Examples could include: female guards in a prison for female offenders, a male restroom attendant for a men's restroom, or a female actor to play Joan of Arc in a movie. However, even the use of a BFOQ in the previous jobs could be the topic of debate. Customer preference does not constitute a BFOQ. Thus, a BFOQ could not be established by simply arguing that customers calling into First Rollins Bank prefer to hear a female sounding voice on the other end of the phone.

Disparate impact occurs when an otherwise neutral device results in adverse impact toward a protected group, and that otherwise neutral device cannot be shown to be job related. Adverse impact refers to a finding of a significant difference in the proportion of minorities, or protected class members, receiving some treatment, for example being hired, as compared to majority group members. There are a variety of statistical rules which can be used to establish the presence of adverse impact including the 80% rule and a 2 to 3 standard deviation rule. The 80% rule of thumb involves comparing the selection rate for a minority group to a selection rate for a majority group. The selection rate is defined as the number selected divided by the number of applicants. If the minority selection rate is less than 80% of the rate for the majority group, then this can be considered as evidence of adverse impact.

As an example of adverse impact, a typing test administered to candidates for the Customer Service Representative job results in a passing rate of 50% for White job candidates, 50 pass out of 100 test takers, and 25% for African-American candidates, 5 out of 20. The adverse impact ratio is 50% (i.e., the passing rate for African-Americans divided by the passing rate for Whites equals .25/.50, or 50%). Since 50% is less than the 80% established by rule, the conclusion is that the typing test does have adverse impact which works against African-American job candidates. However, if the typing test can be shown to be job related, usually through a content validation study, then the conclusion would be that the test has adverse impact but is not discriminatory.

The 2 to 3 standard deviation rule can be operationalized using the z test which is available in most statistical packages. If the minority and majority selection rates differ by more than 2 to 3 standard units, then this is considered to represent statistical evidence of adverse impact.

A test, or other selection device, which results in adverse impact is not necessarily discriminatory. The device can still be used if it is shown to be job related. The major method for demonstrating the job relatedness of a selection device is a validation study. The formal requirements for validation studies are listed in the Uniform Guidelines issued by the Equal Employment Opportunity Commission (EEOC). However, this is a technical topic, and unless you have sufficient sophistication in this area, you should probably contact an industrial psychologist who specializes in validation studies.

The classic example of disparate impact involves the case of *Griggs vs. Duke Power Company*, a landmark hiring case which was settled by the United States Supreme Court in 1971. In the years following the Civil Rights Acts of 1964, Duke Power Company began to require that employees in certain job classes have a High School Diploma and pass general aptitude tests. This had a disparate impact on blacks because they often had less formal education and fewer blacks than whites were able to pass the test. In ruling in favor of Griggs, the court established the principle that if a requirement for employment, including tests and minimum qualifications, resulted in adverse impact, then there must be evidence that the selection device was professionally developed and job related.

As a recruiter, you also need to be aware that certain questions which seem neutral may result in or be interpreted as resulting in disparate impact (of course, it is also possible that in some cases the questions could be seen as offering evidence for a finding of disparate treatment). Some examples would include:

❖ Have you ever been arrested?
❖ Do you own a car?
❖ What is your native tongue?
❖ What country did your family come from?
❖ Where were you born?

❖ Are you married?

❖ Are you divorced?

❖ Are you engaged?

❖ Does your family mind if you travel?

❖ Who will care for your children while you work?

❖ Do you plan on becoming pregnant?

❖ What is your spouse's job?

❖ Does your spouse have health coverage?

❖ Shouldn't you be retiring soon?

❖ Aren't you too old to go through any more training programs?

Again, the type of questions which may be problematic may vary by state. As a result, we would advise you to check with an employment law expert regarding any problems which might be encountered.

During the interview, some job candidates may voluntarily disclose inappropriate information. Some examples include the job candidate who says:

❖ *"Oh, I left my last position at Big State University because I became involved with a faculty member. I had to get a divorce. It was awful. Let me tell you about it..."*

❖ *"The reason I have that one year gap between jobs is that I had a child. She is so beautiful. Here, I just got back a whole roll of pictures. Let me show them to you."*

❖ *"I love to travel, but I wonder what I will do about child care. My kids have a lot of soccer games. My son scored a goal yesterday..."*

This is a difficult situation to deal with in an appropriate manner. You do not want to be rude. However, you also do not want to hear additional information which could come back to haunt you if a discrimination lawsuit is filed. Our advice is to return to the basic principles — take control. In order to reestablish control, you should avoid responding to the person's story, other than perhaps some appropriate body language to show that you are listening but want to move on to other topics. Without discussing the content of the story, you should simply indicate that:

> *"If you don't mind, I do need to get some more information from you. Let's return to another question."*

Federal Agencies

The two major federal agencies charged with enforcing equal employment laws are the Equal Employment Opportunity Commission (EEOC) and the Office of Federal Contract Compliance Programs (OFCCP). Most states also have their own fair employment commission for the purpose of enforcing state equal employment laws.

The EEOC deals with violations of Title VII of the Civil Rights Act. They process complaints of discrimination and, as a result of their investigation, may find that there is reasonable cause to believe that a violation has occurred. As an independent regulatory agency, the EEOC also issues written regulations governing employment practices, including their guidelines on selection procedures which are commonly referred to as the *EEOC Uniform Guidelines*. Through EEO-1 forms, the EEOC also gathers information or data on employment patterns by race and sex.

The OFCCP deals primarily with federal contractors and with the enforcement of Executive Orders. In practice, the OFCCP is closely identified with the notion of affirmative action and with the development of affirmative action plans. The topic of affirmative action will be discussed in more detail later in this chapter.

Protected Classes and Federal Laws

Human resource professionals, and others involved in recruiting, should be familiar with the implications for hiring practices of the following pieces of legislation:

❖ The Civil Rights Act of 1964 and 1991
❖ The Age Discrimination in Employment Act of 1967
❖ The American with Disabilities Act of 1990

The major piece of legislation dealing with discrimination in hiring is Title VII of the Civil Rights Act of 1964 which has since been amended on a number of occasions (Equal Employment Opportunity Act of 1972, The Civil Rights Act of 1991). The Civil Rights Act covers discrimination due to race, color, religion, sex and national origin. Somewhat surprisingly, to some, the Civil Rights Act does not require that an employer make good or rational decisions.

In general, equal employment and nondiscrimination policies are aimed at particular, identifiable groups, with the two major areas of concern being the detection and elimination of race and sex discrimination. Information on sex and race has usually been collected through self-report, where individuals are asked to fill out a form where they check the most appropriate racial or ethnic category. The five categories (at the present time, consideration is being given to changing the five basic categories) used for reporting race, or ethnicity, are:

1. American Indian or Alaskan Native
2. Asian or Pacific Islander
3. Black
4. White
5. Hispanic

There is no requirement in Title VII that an employer maintain a racial balance in the work force. Any deliberate attempt to maintain a racial balance could be construed as reverse discrimination. Furthermore, The Civil

Rights Act of 1991 specifically prohibited certain types of race norming and other score adjustments based on race or sex.

Title VII also offers protection against discrimination based on religion. However, the effect of Title VII is somewhat muted by the First Amendment to the Constitution. The prohibition against discrimination based on religion is probably more important to employers in areas such as retail sales, where the issue of Saturday and Sunday work arises, than it is to employment law experts. In general, practices such as Sunday work rules that adversely affect certain religious groups are allowable if the employer is unable to reasonably accommodate without an undue hardship. Although it is acceptable to ask whether a person can work the required hours or shifts, questions should be avoided on religious practices or on the observance of religious holidays.

Title VII of the Civil Rights Act does *not* cover age discrimination. Age discrimination is covered by the Age Discrimination in Employment Act of 1967 (ADEA), which protects individuals 40 years of age and older. Some states have enacted laws which also protect younger individuals, or may cover other age ranges, so again it would be appropriate to check on laws which apply to the individual states for which you are recruiting.

While age discrimination is probably more likely to be a factor in promotions, layoffs, or retirement decisions, discrimination based on age can occur in recruitment. An obvious example would be when a company imposes age limits on new hires (i.e., the company will not hire anyone over the age of 40 as a new employee). Thus, any selection processes should be audited for procedures which may result in age discrimination or make age a factor; this would include the use of questions during the interview which might reflect an age bias.

Physical or mental disabilities are covered by the Americans with Disabilities Act of 1990 (ADA). At this point, the exact implications of this act for the recruitment process are still difficult to pinpoint, as there have been insufficient court cases to define the applications of the Act. Another problem with discussing applications of this Act is that unlike other Civil Rights legislation, the ADA it is clearly aimed at individuals and individual accommodation rather than at groups. Under the ADA, employers must be aware of the general principle of "reasonable accommodation," (i.e., employers must make a reasonable accommodation unless the employer can demonstrate that such an accommodation would impose an undue hardship on the business — the larger the organization, the harder it would be to prove undue hardship).

During the interview, questions should be avoided which address general physical impairments. For example, the following question would be inappropriate:

❖ *"Your legs look kind of thin. Do you have any leg problems?"*

All questions should be job related and tied to major or essential job duties. Thus, an appropriate question might be:

❖ *"This job requires dealing with customers for 8 hours a day. In order to deal with customers, you must spend a lot of time walking and standing on hard, concrete floors. Would you be able to do that?"*

The interpretation of the ADA appears to be in a state of flux. As a result, we would recommend consulting any recent guidelines concerning the ADA which might have been issued by the EEOC and/or recent court cases.

In addition to the protected classes listed above, a number of federal laws, state laws, or executive orders exist which cover other groups including veterans and immigrants. Laws also exist covering areas such as salary and sexual harassment.

Affirmative Action

Affirmative action refers to procedures which attempt to increase the representation of an underrepresented, protected group (for a more advanced discussion of the issues involved in affirmative action see the book by Doverspike, Taylor, and Arthur, 1999, *Affirmative Action: A Psychological Perspective*). Although there are many different definitions of affirmative action, and the operationalization of affirmative action is a topic which can lead to heated debates, the OFCCP offers an administrative definition of affirmative action. Under OFCCP regulations, certain organizations receiving federal contracts must maintain an affirmative action plan. This plan must contain information on how the plan is maintained, reporting and internal auditing systems, support for community action programs, and compliance with nondiscrimination guidelines. In addition, organizations must conduct an analysis to identify underrepresentation. This analysis includes a workforce analysis, availability analysis, utilization analysis, a statement of goals, and a statement of progress toward goals. The purpose of this workforce analysis is to identify underrepresentation based upon a comparison of minority availability to minority hiring. If underutilization exists, the company can set goals in order to rectify any problem areas which are identified. If the organization is required to maintain an affirmative action plan, then human resource professionals, as well as other employees involved in recruiting, should be familiar with their organization's affirmative action plan.

The recruitment of minorities and other members of protected classes often represents a special challenge for organizations. Companies frequently describe themselves as being equal employment opportunity employers or affirmative action employers, however, very little is known concerning the effects of such self identification on recruitment efforts or even what such self identification actually implies. Although an organizational emphasis on diversity issues and affirmative action should increase the attractiveness of an organization, this seems to vary as a function of whether the organization also places an emphasis on merit. As a result, organizations should emphasize the merit and competency of those beneficiaries brought in under affirmative action programs, as this will help to increase the perceived attractiveness of the employer and will also decrease resistance from those organizational members whose opposition stems from negative beliefs about the competency of minorities or of other members of protected groups. Thus, while encouraging employers to implement appropriate and legal affirmative action efforts, we also believe that by placing an emphasis on the basic principles, the five hurdles, and creating a climate of achievement, organizations can increase their hit rate in recruiting both minority and majority group members.

Testing

Anyone involved with employment testing should have some basic knowledge of the professional principles and legal guidelines which apply to the use of selection procedures. The following are basic references that recruiters should at least be familiar with:

1. *Standards for Educational and Psychological Testing* (APA, 1999). From the American Psychological Association, this document presents professional standards for constructing and using all types of tests. The 1999 edition replaced an earlier version and was issued as this book was going to press.

2. *Principles for the Validation and Use of Personnel Selection Procedures* (DIV 14, 1987). From Division 14, the Industrial-Organizational Psychology division of the American Psychological Association, this document covers the professional standards for the construction, validation, and use of employment tests.

3. *Uniform Guidelines on Employee Selection Procedures* (EEOC, 1978). From the Equal Employment Opportunity Commission of the United States Government, this document presents the basic principles of selection and testing.

4. *Interpretation and Clarification of Uniform Employee Selection Guidelines* (1979). Also from the Equal Employment Opportunity Commission, this document supplements the original *Guidelines*.

There are also a number of textbooks which are available on testing issues. A standard reference which is relatively easy to read is Cascio's (1998) *Applied Psychology in Human Resource Management*. Other selected texts are listed in the reference section.

The critical principle to keep in mind is that tests, and other selection devices, should be reliable, valid and job related. Procedures or guidelines for validating tests are provided in the *EEOC Uniform Guidelines* and in books such as Cascio's. Firms which provide tests should also be able to assist in developing the appropriate documentation for demonstrating the job relatedness or validity of their instruments. If professional assistance is needed, industrial psychologists specialize in the validation of tests for employment purposes.

Summary

In this chapter, a number of extremely complicated issues have been covered very briefly. Employment law is a complex, specialized area. We would encourage the interested reader to attend any of the excellent training sessions offered in many states on complying with civil rights legislation. If in doubt, contact qualified, legal professionals. The best defense is not ignorance but knowledge.

In addition to knowledge, the two simple rules we can offer you are:

❖ Document everything. Document your methods, processes, and decisions. Document when a search process starts and when it ends.

❖ Be consistent. Treat applicants in a fair and consistent manner. If you have methods, processes, or rules, then be sure to follow them in the same manner with every candidate.

9

Special Issues

his chapter is intended primarily for the human resource professional. In the first part of the chapter, we discuss the application of
the basic principles to some special groups and situations. First, we
deal with the employer of choice, where the recruit-as-customer argument
appears to have originated. Second, we discuss the unique challenges, and
advantages, of recruiting in the public sector. Third, we look at a group which
has garnered its fair share of media attention – Generation X. In the second
part of this chapter, we illustrate how the basic principles can be applied to
the management of a career in human resources.

Employers of Choice

One of the rationales for this book, was that much of what was currently
being written by others on recruitment was based on companies which
were already leaders in their respective fields. The organizations being used
as examples were employers of choice, companies which had an extremely
positive image, offered the top salaries, offered excellent benefits, and had
the flexibility and resources, including being able to pay large signing bo-
nuses, to attract top performers away from their competitors. For employers of choice, simply being offered a job by the organization can go a long
way toward fulfilling an individual's needs for achievement, power and
affiliation. The employer does not need to create or maintain an image,
they already have the image others are striving to attain.

As a result, some employers of choice have moved toward the adoption of a version of the recruitment process where the job candidate is viewed as a customer, a customer who is pampered not challenged. If a company has reached the lofty status where the job candidate can be treated as a customer, and the recruit-as-customer approach works for the company, then we have no problem with that strategy. In fact, we have argued that recruitment is situational, that the processes and methods which work best will depend upon the situation, with the procedures we have described in this book working particularly well in the case of the hard to fill or difficult hire. Nevertheless, although the exact methods used by employers of choice may vary, the underlying philosophy adopted by the human resource professional must remain the same. That is, the recruiter remains the most important ingredient in successful hiring (Basic Principle 1).

Recruiting in the Public Sector

The issues involved in recruiting in the public sector do appear to be substantially different from those encountered by private organizations dealing with hard to fill positions. Although some positions in the public sector, such as those in the areas of information technology and health care related positions, may be hard to fill, prime positions in the public sector, such as firefighter and police officer, still appear to attract a large number of job candidates, sometimes in excess of 10,000 candidates. As a result, the problem for public sector personnel management professionals is often one of how to deal with too many applicants, rather than too few.

In many ways, the procedures described in this book, if not the philosophy, are already used in the public sector. However, the problem in the public sector is often one of requiring job applicants to jump over too many hurdles, rather than too few. The hiring process often takes too much time rather than being too rushed. The required solution in the public sector may not be one that involves attracting more applicants, but may instead demand speeding up and simplifying the process.

Although the methods may vary, the underlying philosophy which must be adopted by the human resource professional is the same. Thus, the basic principles remain the same, even if the methods for implementing or improving the recruitment process change. The recruiter's attitude remains the most important ingredient in successful hiring.

Generation X

According to the popular media and human resources journals, Generation X, a demographic group consisting of those individuals born between 1965 and 1980, presents a special and unusual recruiting challenge. Popular descriptions of Generation X describe its members as:

❖ Envying previous generations for the opportunities that were available in their time.

❖ Having family relationships which are characterized by a great deal of separation including divorced, single, and step parents.

❖ Being more spiritual and tolerant but less religious.

❖ From a vocational perspective, holding McJobs, which are characterized by low pay, low status, feelings of dissatisfaction with employment prospects, and career instability. At the same time, Generation Xers are also described as having a high need for achievement, variety, growth, and intellectual stimulation.

❖ In terms of benefits, being less interested in group based pay schemes and family friendly policies.

Based on our own program of research, we have found that some of the popular perceptions are accurate and some are less than accurate. In relation to vocational preferences, Generation Xers, as compared to other adults, are more likely to believe that they will not hold the same job for more than a year. This finding may indicate a desire for variety or it may simply indicate a disappointment with one's current McJob and a desire to move into a better one. Generation Xers tend to prefer to start with a high base salary and place less value on benefits such as pay-for-performance, vacation time, and family friendly benefits. It should be noted, that this may partially reflect the age of Generation Xers, as much as it does any unique societal or developmental process. Younger workers, in general, tend to place less value on benefits such as retirement and health insurance policies.

As part of our research, we also developed an instrument which measures the degree to which an individual identifies with Generation X. Statistical analyses of this measure indicate that the dimensions which differentiate Generation X include:

❖ Attitudes toward religion (more spiritual and less traditional).
❖ Body Art (tattoos and piercings).
❖ Preferences in movies and music (Nirvana).
❖ Computer literacy and use (use of e-mail, etc.).

Overall, although at times Generation Xers have been described as slackers, they appear to have a strong need for achievement. This would suggest that Generation Xers would respond very favorably to any recruitment effort which emphasizes high standards and the creation of a climate of achievement. As a result, the basic principles would appear to provide the proper foundation for designing recruitment programs which are aimed at Generation X.

Managing Your Career in Human Resources

If you are or wish to become a human resource professional, the basic principles can be applied, not only to recruiting, but also to your daily working relationships with peers, supervisors, subordinates, and other employees in the organization (For more details on working with managers, see Chapter 10). Controlling perceptions is just as important in managing your own career as it is in recruiting.

As a concrete step toward building a better future, a prototypical career path analysis should be conducted based upon where you would like to be in ten years. Then, the Prototypical Career Path analysis can be compared to your own career path. Based upon this comparison, you should be able to identify what you are doing right and where your weaknesses are. For example, if you have been in human resources for several years, you might end up asking yourself a series of questions including:

❖ Have I been promoted?
❖ Have I taken additional courses or training to improve my knowledge base?
❖ Have I considered additional education?
❖ Have I joined professional groups such as the *Society for Human Resource Management?*
❖ Have I established the types of alliances with managers I need to establish in order to be effective?
❖ Have I been applying the basic principles to both recruiting and my daily relationships at work?

Once you have identified the discrepancies between where you should be and where your career is currently, then you can develop an action plan in order to begin to remedy any deficiencies.

If you are a supervisor, or have a chance to serve as a supervisor, then many of the principles discussed here for recruiting can also be applied to the supervision of employees. Survey research conducted in organizational settings consistently finds that supervisors are the most important factor in determining their subordinates', attitudes. Your perceptions will become your subordinates'; perceptions. If you are also in the position where you are supervising other recruiters, then your attitude will be reflected in their attitudes. Consider the supervisor of ten full-time recruiters. Each recruiter has contact with 1,000 job candidates a year. The supervisor, through the effect of the supervisor's attitude and behaviors on the recruiters, has an impact on 10,000 job candidates per year. This is a tremendous responsibility and also illustrates how by changing your own perception you can begin to change the face of the whole organization and also begin to meet your own career goals.

Summary

This chapter was devoted to a discussion of several issues which may be of special interest to the human resource professional. Although the recruiter remains the most important determinant of successful recruiting (Basic Principle 1), the methods and basic principles discussed in this book may require further modification when applied to either employers of choice or the public sector. Generation Xers would appear to be particularly receptive to the type of climate of achievement which is created through the application of the basic principles and the five hurdles. Finally, the basic principles can be applied in working with peers, supervisors, subordinates, and other employees in the organization.

10

The New Face of the Organization

If you follow the basic principles, you will be changing the face of the organization. Your company will begin to have a new image. The new hires will have a new attitude and a new outlook on their jobs and on their futures with the organization. The whole organization will begin to change. Our experience has been that it takes about nine months to begin to see the results. Hopefully, you will see the following:

❖ Increased morale and job satisfaction which should lead to reduced turnover.

❖ Increased job performance due to the caliber of employee being hired by the organization.

❖ Managers will find themselves having to adapt new leadership styles in order to effectively supervise the new type of employee. They will find that their job is much easier and that they are receiving the type of employee who matches the manager's preferred leadership styles and goals.

❖ Improved customer service and sales (depending upon the nature of the business) because your organization will be perceived in a more favorable light by outsiders and because they will be receiving better products and service.

Over time, the reputation of your company should continue to improve, hopefully to the point where you become an employer of choice.

Unfortunately, change is sometimes difficult to accept and may be met with resistence. Next we'll look at various methods for dealing with resistence from both employees hired under the old methods and from managers in the organization. Although this chapter was primarily written for human resource professionals, especially the section on "Working with Managers," the information here should be of interest to all readers.

Dealing With Resistance From Employees

One likely source of resistance to change will be employees who were hired under the old methods and thinking. These employees will feel challenged by the new methods and by the attitudes and performance of the new hires. They may feel inadequate compared to the new employees hired under higher standards.

Some of the older employees may choose to leave the organization. As a result, over the first nine months of the implementation of our basic principles, the organization may experience a short term increase in turnover. You should be prepared for this increase, but realize that in the long run it will benefit the organization.

TECHNICAL NOTE: The psychological construct which is used to refer to the judgment of the fairness of an intervention independent of its effect on personal outcomes is *procedural justice*. The degree to which an individual personally benefits from an intervention is referred to as *distributive justice*. Both procedural and distributive justice affect attitudinal reactions to an intervention. A third factor which has an important influence on how satisfied a person is with an intervention is the communications they receive from other individuals regarding their opinions on the fairness of intervention.

For the employees who choose to stay, one radical idea is to involve them in the change process. Through training or other types of organizational communication, the human resource department should keep current employees informed of the changes and show them that the improvements are in the best interest of everyone involved. When people feel a sense of involvement, they are more likely to view an intervention as fair even if they do not experience personal benefit.

Working With Managers

In order to be an effective recruiter, you must establish and maintain a positive working relationship with managers in the company, especially line managers. If a recruiter does have a customer, it is the hiring manager. You must meet the needs of the manager at the same time you are meeting the needs of the job candidate.

Step five of the selection hurdles is an interview between the manager, or supervisor, and the job candidate. It does no one any good when a job candidate passes all of the other hurdles, but is rejected by the manager. A climate of trust must be developed and nurtured between the recruiter and the managers. The greater the trust, the more likely it is that the manager will agree with your decisions and view you as a member of the management team. In addition, if a manager trusts the recruiter, then the manager is more likely to start with a positive first impression of a job candidate. As a recruiter, you want to get to the point where the managers will say to themselves, *"I do not know much about these job candidates, but if Pat Davis is sending them to me, then they must be very good."*

In dealing with managers, please remember that you are a competent professional. In theory, you are the expert in recruiting and possess the answers and solutions to a myriad of human resource problems. All too often, we encounter recruiters who see their job as one of simply shuffling resumes so as to find a few potential candidates for the manager to interview. If that is your current attitude, it is the wrong attitude and you need to change it. Computer programs exist which can identify potential candidates from resumes. Your job is not simply one of dredging up job candidates for managers to select. As a recruiter, you are responsible for helping to identify and select a new type of employee, one who will help to change the face of the organization. Once you have established that self image in your own mind, then you can begin to convert it into action so that others will also see you as a competent professional. In order to meet tight hiring deadlines and the increased volume of paperwork found in human resources, it is critically important that you work hard, pay attention to details, and stay organized.

Of course, if you perform your job well, it will be much easier to create the perception of a competent professional. When problems do occur, the affected managers will be more likely to excuse your errors. If you do make a mistake, then you should take responsibility and apologize for the error. If possible, a solution to the error should be found and implemented. If you do make errors, then be sure to learn from your mistakes.

In human resources, you will have access to a wealth of confidential information — including salaries and who is getting laid off — on the company and on job candidates. It is imperative that you maintain the confidentiality of all data to which you have access. This includes confidential information you receive from managers in the organization.

Life in organizations is often highly political. However, you should make it your practice to avoid getting involved in political disputes. If someone upsets you, then either address the problem or forget it and move on; it is not always possible to be everyone's friend. The habit of attacking managers behind their back should be avoided. The viewpoint should be adopted that the managers in the organization should be respected in that they are hard working and trying to accomplish the company's goals.

In working with managers, communication should be one of the main priorities. Managers should be kept informed as to the results and progress throughout each step of the hiring process. For correspondence regarding routine issues, memorandums, email, and voice mail should be used instead of personal telephone calls, which consume the valuable time of both parties. However, when a manager does indicate that there is a problem or expresses a concern, the best response is to deal directly with that individual either by phone or in person.

Although it is not necessary, nor possible, that you become an expert in every field for which you recruit, you should become knowledgeable in the basic lingo of different occupational areas. However, if you are technically ignorant in an area, you should admit it and be willing to learn.

Managers and supervisors will have their own personalities and needs and also their own perceptions of what constitutes an ideal candidate. You do not need a degree in psychology to start to become aware of what type of employee is preferred by various managers. As a way of forming a rough categorization scheme, managers can be divided up into those whose style of leadership is based upon:

❖ Working with people. This corresponds to the need for affiliation and also the Big Five personality factors of agreeableness and, in part, extroversion.

❖ An emphasis on processes and/or production. This corresponds to a need for achievement and also the Big Five personality factors of conscientiousness and, in part, extroversion.

❖ An emphasis on ideas. This corresponds to a need for variety and intellectual stimulation and also the Big Five personality factor of openness.

In general, managers will be happiest when the employees they receive from human resources have personality and styles which are similar to their own, although at times they will be looking for a subordinate whose personality style supplements their own. For example, a manager who emphasizes performance through production may want an assistant manager who is best at working with people. If you have never recruited for a particular manager before, and are unfamiliar with their style, then give them a call or sit down in person and review their perceptions of the ideal candidate. As a recruiter, your job is not limited to finding the candidate with the perfect skills for the job, you must also find candidates who can work with and for the supervisor or manager.

If you are in human resources, there are additional steps which you can take in order to maintain a good working relationship with the managers in your company. Remember, we all have a need for achievement and for affiliation. When a manager obtains a promotion, you should send an appropriate message of congratulations and indicate your eagerness to work with him or her in their new capacity. At the same time, you should identify what was it about the manager that led to receiving the promotion. This information will be useful in the future when you are creating prototypical career paths.

A critical link in the organizational chain of command is the secretary. You will need the assistance of secretaries in scheduling candidates' visits and interviews. The secretary will probably meet with the candidates, formally or informally. On occasion, candidates will report spending more time with the manager's secretary than with the manager. Depending upon the manager, the secretary may provide input regarding the final hiring decision. As a result, you should always treat secretaries with the respect they deserve and have earned. In addition to being an important factor in shaping a candidate's perceptions, secretaries can also help the recruiter to cover up for their mistakes and rectify their errors.

Dealing With Resistance From Managers

Even if you do your job effectively, you may face resistance from other organizational members including managers and supervisors. Oftentimes, organizations employ rather laissez faire methods of recruiting and hiring which allow managers significant latitude in decision making. As a result, some managers may resist the introduction of new recruiting and screening methods which they may see as leading to a reduction in their power.

Interventions are more likely to be accepted and seen as fair when the affected managers, and employees, are informed of the reasons for change and given a change to voice their concerns over the changes – the concept of procedural justice. Therefore, you need to make sure that communication channels are open and remain open. Communications can be accomplished through a meeting or through whatever medium will reach the target audience most effectively and efficiently — newsletters, memorandums, or email. Early on, you should try to get the various parties involved to agree that there is a problem. By gaining agreement that a problem exists, the door is opened for consideration of solutions. You should be willing to accept suggestions and feedback, as well as provide any information which is requested by managers. In implementing selection methods, make sure that the managers involved understand that their preferences will be considered in designing screening techniques.

When talking with resistors, try to apply some of the psychological principles from the discussion of the interview (See Chapter 4). Our experience has been that all too often people associate change in their organization with layoffs or pay cuts. When employees hear that a consultant has been brought in or that an organizational change is taking place, their first thought is to wonder whether their job is at stake. Therefore, in communicating with managers, listen not just for the content of the message, but also for the feeling which underlies the message. Listen for the process as well as the content. When a manager says to you, *"I oppose this program because it is too costly,"* they may really be saying, *"I oppose this program because it will eliminate my department and I fear for my own job and the jobs of my subordinates."* Successful managers are often high in their need for power and, as a result, often fear that a reorganization will reduce their power in the organization.

A major reason for resistence is the failure to see the value in a new procedure, so be ready to explain the benefits and advantages of the new recruiting methods. When discussing potential benefits, you should use phrases which speak directly to a manager's need for achievement, such as:

❖ *"Let's raise our level of performance."*
❖ *"We should hire the best we can hire."*
❖ *"We need to be the best organization we can be."*

As a way of responding to the need for affiliation, managers can be organized into subgroups where they can share their experiences regarding the effects of changes.

A key to success for any type of organizational intervention is obtaining top level commitment. Once you receive top level commitment, be sure to publicize it. In addition, alliances should be created with those managers who support you and your programs.

If all else fails, and we do not believe it will, then try to change behaviors, even if you cannot change attitudes. Although we would prefer to change attitudes and then behaviors, changing behaviors can lead to a change in attitudes.

Finally, managers love to see data. If possible, the human resource department should put a mechanism into place for evaluating the results of the adoption of the new philosophy for recruiting the difficult hire.

The Best of All Worlds

It is of course possible that you might not encounter any resistance from within your organization. While it may seem unlikely, on a number of occasions recently we have found opposition to change to be minimal. Potential resistance is reduced by the tight labor market.

The reason that many of you may have picked up a book on difficult hires is that your organization is in a time of crises where, due to its inability to recruit, the company has reached the *"We'll try anything"* stage. Managers are looking for any recruiting method which will deliver qualified hires. So, the potential for resistance to change has already been reduced by the crisis created by market conditions. This creates an optimal situation for introducing your new solution consisting of the seven basic principles, the five hurdles, and the prototypical career path method.

If you follow the basic principles, the face of the organization will begin to change. However, change is not an easy process and is often met with resistence. The best way to deal with potential resistence is to be aware of it, prepared for it, and open in your dealings with managers and employees. If you have followed the basic principles, then you will have developed a positive image of yourself, the company, and the jobs in the company. The next step then is to communicate this attitude to the managers and employees in the company; as you have done in your role as a recruiter – control the perceptions. Always remember, even those resistant employees and managers are potential recruiters.

11

Concluding Thoughts

The word *recruit* means to raise, to strengthen, to revive, and to restore. As a recruiter, you are in the position to change and revitalize your organization by hiring quality people. You are also in the position of being able to change the lives of many individuals by finding them employment which brings financial and personal satisfaction to them and to their families. This is an awesome responsibility.

In order to handle this responsibility, you need to believe in yourself and your organization. The image the job candidate develops of the company and the job will depend upon you and your attitude. You are the most important factor in recruiting and in making those difficult hires.

Hopefully, you can now see how important the right attitude and the right mind set are to your future success as a recruiter. That is why this book has really been about the recruiter's attitudes and about certain basic principles which can be adopted in order to create the proper attitude. There are a number of other fine books which are available on the technology of recruiting, and we would certainly encourage you to seek out other sources on recruiting methods, but this book has really been about attitude and philosophy.

If you have just finished reading this book for the first time, we would recommend that you read through it a second time. This time as you read the book concentrate on how you perceive yourself, your company, and the jobs within the company. Are the images positive ones? If not, then you need to try to visualize a more positive image and then internalize that more positive image.

As you read through the book the second time, try to think of the differences between where you are now in terms of your outlook toward recruiting and the jobs you try to fill and where you need to be to effectively recruit for hard to fill positions. Based on the discrepancies you identify, create a list of goals for yourself. Then, go out and turn those goals into effective action.

Still Having Trouble

If you have tried following the basic principles and are still having trouble finding employees for hard to fill positions, then ask yourself three questions:

1. *"Have I placed the job and the company where it should be — on a pedestal?"*

2. *"Are my standards set high enough for the candidates to perceive getting a job offer to be a MAJOR accomplishment?"*

3. *"Am I really following the seven basic principles, or have I gone back to my old methods and old approaches?"*

If your answer to any of the questions above is *no*, then you need to take a deeper look at why it is that you are having trouble changing your perceptions or standards.

Anytime we change our attitudes and behaviors, we have to give up old, well learned, and familiar habits. When our new path becomes blocked, we often revert back to the old methods or our old behaviors. This return to our old attitudes and behaviors is referred to as *relapse*.

Unfortunately, relapse is an all too common phenomenon. Consider the following two familiar situations:

❖ You have gone on a diet to lose a few pounds and for the past week have done a good job of sticking to your diet. You have a lousy day and work, and when you come home you go to get a glass of water out of the refrigerator. Upon opening the refrigerator, you see a big piece of chocolate cake. The cake is hard to resist and you cannot help yourself — you eat the cake. At this point, you have relapsed into your old behavior. The real problem at this point is not that you have relapsed, but that you will feel guilty or ashamed for slipping. Your image of yourself switches from someone who is sticking to a diet to an image of a person who can never stick to a diet. In response to your guilt, you decide to make yourself a nice, big roast beef sandwich. Of course, this is exactly what you do not want to do. What you need to do is to learn how to handle the relapse and not make it worse by returning full-time to your old behaviors.

❖ If you are more comfortable with sport's analogies, consider trying to change your putting grip in golf (for those readers with limited familiarity with the fine points of the game of golf, putting describes the stroke a golfer makes in order to hit the ball into the hole from only a few feet away). For the first week, the new grip works well, but then you miss a few putts. You become uncomfortable and switch back to your old grip. You make the next putt and feel good about having made it, although a little guilty for giving up on the new grip. The right thing to do would be to go back to using your new grip, but human nature often dictates sticking with the old, familiar grip.

How can you fight relapse, whether in dieting, your golf grip, or in your new attitude toward recruiting? A simple principle of learning is that it is important to continue to practice what we have learned. Furthermore, in order to avoid slipping back into bad habits, it is necessary to develop coping strategies for avoiding and overcoming threats to the newly learned behaviors. More specifically, you can fight the relapse into old habits through:

❖ Simple awareness of the relapse process.
❖ Developing a positive self image and belief in yourself.
❖ Realizing why it is you are trying to switch.
❖ Identifying situations which may lead to a relapse.
❖ Setting goals or targets.
❖ Establishing a support system.

If you recognize that relapse is a natural process, then you will not feel as guilty when you do slip back into your old attitudes or habits. You will realize that relapse is not a result of some personal flaw, but that it is a common phenomena whenever an individual is attempting to learn something new. Thus, the correct response to a relapse is not to slip further but rather to recognize what is occurring and to return as quickly as possible to the newly learned attitudes or behaviors.

Perceptions are important and you should have a positive image of yourself and your company. You need to see yourself as a professional, who is more than capable of setting and maintaining high standards. It does not mean that you have suddenly become less competent, simply because you slip back into old attitudes or behaviors.

In fighting relapse, it is helpful if you remind yourself of the reasons why it is that you are trying to switch from the old approach to the new. If necessary, you should sit down and make a list for yourself of the costs and benefits of the old versus the new behavior. In the case of recruiting, remember all of the problems you had in the past with hard to fill positions and also remember why it was that you originally looked for an alternative to your old methods. Then, think of all the potential benefits you and your company will receive as a result of the adoption of a new attitude toward recruiting.

In order to be prepared for potential relapse, you can identify the circumstances which may lead to relapse and then develop plans for avoiding those situations. For example, you might feel that one problem which could lead to a return to old methods of recruiting would be time pressures. Then, you should identify potential solutions to the problem which would help to avoid the problem and prevent any slippage. For example, perhaps time pressures exist because you are not sufficiently organized – the solution would be to improve your organizational skill. In analyzing the source or cause of a problem, it is also worth considering that many problems do not stem from a single source, but may result from a series of small decisions.

Goals or targets should be established related to each new attitude or behavior. A tracking system can be set up in order to monitor performance in relation to the goals which you have established. For example, you might say to yourself *"I am going to start by applying the principles I have learned to the hiring for positions in our call center. For the next 20 openings, I am going to apply the principles I have learned in this book. I will follow the principles and steps in the book with all of the job candidates for those 20 positions. I will make sure that all 20 hires meet the high standards which I will set and are really the type of people we want in our organization. I will track their performance with the organization after they are hired and also contact their supervisors in order to make sure I have really hired high quality people."* We are confident that if you do set the above targets for yourself, you will be satisfied with the results. In addition, other individuals in the organization, including the new hires and their supervisors, will also be satisfied with the results.

People have a need for affiliation. They need support and guidance from other individuals. We all need someone to talk to about our problems and to receive advice from regarding solutions to our problems, whether that other person is another individual in our organization or in another organization. As a means of formalizing a social support system, we often recommend setting up a buddy system. With the buddy system, each recruiter is paired in training, and after training, with another recruiter. The two buddies can then offer social support to each other including offering advice, comparing results, and sometimes simply serving as a sympathetic ear.

If you do not have access to another professional in your organization, then contact your local human resources organization – many communities have branches of the *Society for Human Resource Management, International Personnel Management*, or similar organizations – and considering becoming a member. Not only will joining such a group provide access to advice from other professionals, it is also a good career builder.

Change is difficult and takes time. There is a natural tendency for individuals to want to return to their old habits. One of the best ways to fight this tendency is simply to realize that it may occur, and probably will, but that relapse is a natural phenomenon and is not a reflection on the strength of the individual nor on the efficacy of the newly learned attitudes and behaviors.

Final Summary

Please remember, the key ingredient is perception. You can control perceptions. You can change perceptions. You can make perceptions work for you and your company.

Remember the basic principles. The basic principles are:

1. You are the most important factor in filling the job.
2. You must stay in control.
3. Perceptions are everything and you can change perceptions.
4. Put the company and the job on a pedestal.
5. Control the negatives.
6. You must fulfill the individual's needs.
7. Set and keep your standards high (This is accomplished through the use of the five hurdles).

Finally, for those of you who desire an even simpler version of the basic principles, or would like to turn the principles into a simple statement which you can repeat to yourself on a regular basis, we offer the following:

I am the most important factor in the recruitment process.
I will stay in control.
I will respond to the needs of the candidate.

Good luck with the hiring and recruitment process and good luck with your own career.

Appendix A

Agenda for Sample Training Program

The following is a sample agenda for a one-day training program. This training outline can be modified fairly easily in order to corre spond to either a two- or a half-day program. For a half-day program, we would recommend scheduling a time for a separate session devoted to the topic of ensuring equal employment opportunity.

In delivering a program based upon this book and our basic principles, the trainer should remember that the main objective is to change attitudes and behaviors. Although we are trying to communicate a philosophy and impart knowledge, our main priority is changing perceptions, including changing the recruiter's own perceptions of their importance and efficacy in the recruitment process. Unfortunately, at times, changing attitudes can take time and a lot of hard work. If you meet with opposition during training, then return to Chapter 10 and review the principles on dealing with resistance.

As a trainer, you need to practice the principles of managing percep tions and staying in control. The trainees should see you as both energetic and enthusiastic. If you do not have confidence in yourself and in your material, then your audience will respond negatively to your presentation. The training program should contain multiple opportunities for interpersonal interactions between the trainer and the trainees. You may encounter the problem of trainees using question periods as an opportunity to express their complaints with the company. There is no problem in allowing a limited amount of personal venting, as long as it is marginally related and within the bounds of what is considered reasonable. However, the trainer also needs to exert control and, as soon as possible, turn the conversation back to the topic of recruiting.

In delivering any training program, you need to be organized and prepared. Prior to training, you should develop an agenda and take the time to develop examples which are tailored to your company. Transparencies and handouts should be created in order to help illustrate the basic principles and the five hurdlers (See Table A.1. and A.2. for such content).

It is also wise to be prepared for questions from the audience. You should take the time to reread the book and familiarize yourself with all of the material. On the other hand, if you do not know the answer to a question, then simply admit your need to refresh your knowledge and promise to get back to the group at a later time with the necessary information. If a knowledgeable lawyer is available, you may want to see if they can assist you with the delivery of the equal employment opportunity section.

As part of the training, we recommend the use of role plays. As the name suggests, in a role play, the participants each play, or act out, one of the parts. In that we are dealing primarily with an interaction between a recruiter and a job candidate, each role play will require two people. One participant will play the role of the recruiter and the other trainee will play the role of the job candidate. The content of the role plays can be edited to reflect the nature of your organization.

If the group is small and the room allows, you may divide all of the trainees into pairs. You can then walk around the room and provide feedback, as well as having the players provide feedback to each other (as another option, if you divide the group into three, you can have one person serve as an observer who then provides feedback). The trainees should switch roles half way through the role play, in order to allow everyone the opportunity to be a recruiter.

If the group is large or the room does not allow for the easy movement of the trainees, an alternative technique is to simply have two trainees come forward and act out the role plays in front of the audience of observers. You can then ask the whole group to provide feedback, and after the feedback session, compare the comments received from the audience to your impressions of the role play.

We recommend that training be evaluated. At a minimum, some type of data should be collected on the reactions of the participants to the training program. You should be able to find details on how to evaluate training programs in almost any training textbook.

Sample Outline

8:00-8:15	Introduction to the topic of the Difficult Hire (Lecture, Chapter 1 and Chapter 2)
8:15-8:30	Trainer led discussion on the topic of past experience with difficult hires and hard to fill positions
8:30-9:00	Lecture and initial presentation on the Basic Principles (Chapter 3)
9:00-9:15	Questions and discussion on the Basic Principles
9:15-9:30	Break
9:30-10:00	Lecture on Controlling the Initial Contact (Chapter 4)
10:00-10:30	Role Play — Controlling the Initial Contact (Table A.3.)
10:30-11:00	Lecture on Minimum Qualifications, The Five Hurdles and the Prototypical Career Path Model (Chapter 5)
11:00-11:15	Break
11:15-11:45	Lecture on Tests and Testing (Chapter 5)
11:45-12:00	Questions and summary
12:00-12:30	Lunch
12:30-1:00	Lecture on the Selection Interview (Chapter 6)
1:00-1:30	Role Play — Selection Interviews (Table A.4.)
1:30-1:45	Break
1:45-2:15	Lecture on The Close (Chapter 7)
2:15-2:45	Role Play — The Close (Table A.5)
2:45-3:00	Break
3:00-4:00	Ensuring Equal Employment Opportunity (Chapter 8)
4:00-4:15	Questions and discussion
4:15-4:45	Lecture and discussion — Final thoughts (Chapter 10)
4:45-5:00	Evaluation

Table A.1.
Finding the Difficult Hire
(The Basic Principles)

1. You are the most important factor in filling the job.
2. You must stay in control.
3. Put the company and the job on a pedestal.
4. Perceptions are everything and you can change perceptions.
5. Control the negatives.
6. You must fulfill the individual's needs.
7. Set and keep your standards high.

Table A.2.
The Five Hurdles

1. Prescreen and Minimum Qualifications
2. Phone Screen and Initial Interview
3. Standardized Testing
4. Second Interview with Recruiter or HR Director
5. Interview with Appropriate Supervisor or Manager

Table A.3.
Role Play for Initial Contact

Instructions: Have one candidate play the job candidate and the other the recruiter. The job candidate should deliver the appropriate line, and then the recruiter should respond. Do not rush. There is no need to get through all the questions.

1. I sure am glad that you are interested in me. I have really given a lot of thought to the type of job I want. I read a book that said you should make up a list of questions to ask the interviewer, and my list is several pages long. Okay. Let me start with the first

item. When will I get my first promotion? When will I get my first pay raise? When...

2. I love to sell. People tell me I am a natural salesperson. I can sell anything. I have attended at least 10 different training programs on selling.

3. I quit my last job because my boss and I did not get along. Oh well, that is life. But, let me tell you about my favorite boss .....

4. I really like working with people. In my last job, I worked in the mall trying to get people to apply for a credit card. I liked meeting all of the people. I liked helping them fill out forms.

5. I love children. I have five of them. Let me tell you about their last soccer game.

6. I really need a job. You look like you need people. Can I start tomorrow?

7. I still do not think I understand the job. What kind of people are you looking for?

8. How many people have you interviewed so far? How many people are you hiring? Do I have a good chance to get the job?

Table A.4.
Role Play for the Selection Interview

Instructions: Have one candidate play the job candidate and the other the recruiter. The recruiter should ask a question corresponding to each area. The job candidate should then respond. The recruiter should then follow up to make sure to get information on 4WP and in order to make sure they are collecting behavioral information. Do not rush. There is no need to get through all the questions.

Ask a question in order to obtain behavioral information on:

1. Dealing with a customer, who has a complaint.
2. Method of dealing with a conflict with a co-worker.
3. Handling of a very difficult goal.
4. Handling of time pressures.

5. Ability to learn new things.
6. Creativity.
7. Leadership style.
8. Approach to dealing with a difficult to please boss.
9. An unexpected problem.
10. What is their greatest weakness? What have they done in the past in order to deal with this weakness? What do they plan on doing in the future to deal with this weakness?
11. How have they prepared for a career in the field? What will they do in the future to prepare for a career in the field?

12. What they would do if they were asked to work on a holiday because another employee was sick?
13. Where they would like to be in five years? Why? And, how they would get to that point?

Table A.5.
Role Play for the Close

Instructions: Have one candidate play the job candidate and the other the recruiter. The scenario is that you are at the end of one of the sessions and need to set up the next session.

1. It is the end of the initial phone contact with the job candidate. Based upon this contact, you, the recruiter, have decided to have the job candidate come in for the next hurdle, which in this case consists of the testing session. There will be a battery of tests administered by computer.
2. The fourth hurdle is complete. You have interviewed the job candidate, and feel that they may be the right person for the job. The next step will be a meeting with the manager, Fred Newsome.
3. The job candidate has passed all five hurdles. You are offering them the job.

Appendix B

The Newspaper Advertisement

The organization and the job candidate do communicate with each other prior to the first contact between the recruiter and the candidate. We have referred to this phase of the recruitment process as precontact. Although, in recent years, the nature of advertising has changed due to the use of the Internet, alternative media – including radio and cable television – and the greater use of large, display ads, the newspaper employment ad remains a major component in the prescreen. In this Appendix, we are concerned primarily with the application of the basic principles to the traditional newspaper advertisement. For additional information on other approaches to advertising, we recommend that the reader consult *The Employer's Guide to Recruiting on the Internet* by Ray Schreyer and John McCarter, and *Hiring Great People* by Kevin Klinvex, Matt O'Connell, and Christoper Klinvex.

With the traditional newspaper advertisement, the company can begin to shape perceptions and also make an initial statement concerning standards. However, the basic principles are somewhat more difficult to apply to the newspaper advertisement in that the communication is fairly limited and operates only in one direction — from the company directed at the job candidate. This, of course, is why organizations have moved to other types of advertising which offer greater control over the presentation of information.

When skimming the employment section of the newspaper, job seekers tend to operate according to a population stereotype where the size of the advertisement is correlated with the importance and starting salary of the job. Thus, people expect to see smaller advertisements for lower level jobs and larger advertisements for higher level jobs. When an advertisement violates this population stereotype, it is likely to cause confusion in the mind of the job seeker. As a result, jobs which pay less than $35,000, usually are associated with small, in-column advertisements. Then, as the importance of the job increases, the size of the advertisement tends to increase proportionally.

Another issue which needs to be addressed in creating an advertisement is the job title. Companies frequently create unique job titles for a variety of reasons. However, when these company specific job titles are used in an advertisement, it can create a great deal of confusion. It is much more effective to use common, marketplace terminology. For example, if in an advertisement the job title was listed as that of a Product Contract Coordinator, few people would know at first glance whether they were qualified for the job. When the same title is turned into its generic equivalent, Entry Level Marketing, most job seekers would know the nature of the job and be able to determine whether they might be qualified for the position. In composing the advertisement, avoid the use of terms which may suggest an age, race or sex preference. For example, use salesperson instead of salesman.

A topic which is sometimes debated in the human resource literature is whether a company should include its name in an advertisement or, as an alternative, should run blind advertisements. Our recommendation is to include the name of the company in the advertisement, with the possible exception being when the position is still filled by a current employee. Seeing one's own position in the newspaper tends to have a negative effect on the employee's morale.

In designing an advertisement, a simple three paragraph format usually works best. The first paragraph should include a short, positive description of the company and job. The second paragraph should describe the minimum qualifications and abilities required for the job, and may also include a description of the characteristics of an ideal candidate. The third paragraph contains contact information and any other additional information which the company might decide to include, such as salary and benefits. An example of an advertisement for an entry level job, Customer Service Representative, appears in Table B.1. An example of an advertisement for an upper level job, Director of Marketing, appears in Table B.2.

Table B.1.
Advertisement for Entry Level Position

Customer Service Representative

First Rollins Bank is a full service bank and one of the fastest growing financial institutions in the region. We offer an environment where you will be challenged by unique opportunities and where your accomplishments can be appreciated and rewarded. Currently, we are seeking to fill Customer Service Representative positions in our call centers.

We are seeking an individual with a high school degree and a minimum typing speed of 30 words per minute. The individual must have a strong work ethic, a record of job stability, a pleasant phone voice, and a friendly customer service orientation. The ideal candidate will also have previous experience in the banking industry. Afternoon and evening shifts are available.

If you are ready to make a difference with a forward-thinking company, we offer attractive compensation, excellent benefits including a retirement plan, and much more. For consideration, please send your resume to Pat Davis, First Rollins Bank, 355 Banking Row, Rollins, OH 44222. An Equal Opportunity Employer.

Table B.2.
Advertisement for Upper Level Position

Director of Marketing

First Rollins Bank is a full service bank and one of the fastest growing financial institutions in the region. We offer an environment where you will be challenged by unique opportunities, appreciated for your contributions, and rewarded and promoted based upon your accomplishments. If you are seeking a career where you can work with the best in shaping the future of banking, we have an excellent opportunity available for a Director of Marketing.

Qualifications include a Bachelor's degree in Marketing, or a related field, and 5 or more years of previous experience in a management position. The candidate must have exceptional written and oral communication skills, computer proficiency, and business knowledge. The individual selected must also have a track record of multiple, timely promotions and be able to demonstrate success in leading and managing subordinates. The ideal candidate will also have previous experience in managing marketing within a service organization and additional education at the graduate level.

If you are ready to make a difference with a forward-thinking company, we offer attractive compensation, excellent benefits including health, dental, and vision insurance, and a 401K with generous match. For consideration, qualified applicants may send a resume to Pat Davis, First Rollins Bank, 355 Banking Row, Rollins, OH 44222. An Equal Opportunity Employer.

Selected Bibliography

Basic References on Recruitment and Selection

American Psychological Association, and others (1999). *Standards for Educational and Psychological Testing.* Washington, DC: Author.

Arthur, D. (1998). *Recruiting, Interviewing, Selecting & Orienting New Employees. Third Edition.* New York: AMACOM.

Arvey, R. D. & Faley, R. H. (1992). *Fairness in Selecting Employees. Second Edition.* Reading, MA: Addison-Wesley.

Barber, A. E. (1998). *Recruiting Employees: Individual and Organizational Perspectives.* Thousand Oaks, CA: Sage.

Cascio, W. *Applied Psychology in Human Resource Management. Fifth Edition.* Upper Saddle River, NJ: Prentice Hall.

Cronbach, L. J. (1990). *Essentials of Psychological Testing. Fifth Edition.* New York: Harper & Row.

Equal Employment Opportunity Commission (1978). Uniform guidelines on employee selection procedures. *Federal Register, 43,* 38290-38309.

Equal Employment Opportunity Commission, et al. (1979). Interpretation and clarification of Uniform Employee Selection Guidelines. *Federal Register, 44,* 11996-12009.

Equal Employment Opportunity Commission, et al. (1980). Adoption of additional questions and answers to clarify and provide a common interpretation of the Uniform Guidelines on Employee Selection Procedures. *Federal Register, 45*, 29529-29531.

Klinvex, K. C., O'Connell, M. S., & Klinvex, C. P. (1999). *Hiring Great People*. New York: McGraw-Hill.

Maitland, I. (1997). *Recruiting: How to Do It*. London: Cassell.

Schreyer, R. & McCarter, J. (1998). *The Employer's Guide to Recruiting on the Internet*. Manassas Park, VA: Impact.

Society for Industrial and Organizational Psychology, Inc. (1987). *Principles for the Validation and Use of Personnel Selection Procedures. Third Edition*. College Park, MD: Author.

Additional References

Adams, S. (1998). *The Dilbert Future: Thriving on Stupidity in the 21ˢᵗ Century*. New York: HarperCollins.

Adler, N. (1972). *The Underground Stream*. New York: Harper.

American Compensation Assoc. (1996). *Raising the Bar: Using Competencies to Enhance Employee Performance*. Author: Scottsdale, AZ.

American Psychological Association, Committee on Psychological Tests and Assessment. (1996). Statement on the disclosure of test data. *American Psychologist, 51*, 644-648.

Arthur, W. A., Jr., Doverspike, D. & Kuthy, J. E. (1996). Striking gold through a deep-level organization intervention in Ghana's mining industry. *International Journal of Organizational Analysis*. 4, 175-186.

Arthur, W. A., Jr., Doverspike, D., & Barrett, G.V. (1996) Development of a job analysis-based procedure for weighting and combining content-related tests into a single battery. *Personnel Psychology, 49*, 971-985.

Arvey, R. D., Miller, H. E., Gould, R., & Burch, P. (1987). Interview validity for selecting sales clerks. *Personnel Psychology, 40*, 1-12.

Barrett, G. V., Alexander, R. A., Doverspike, D. (1992). The implications for personnel selection of apparent declines in predictive validity over time: A reply to Hulin, Henry & Noon. *Personnel Psychology, 45*, 601-618.

Barrick, M. R., & Mount, M. K. (1991). The big five personality dimensions and job performance: A meta-analysis. *Personnel Psychology, 44*, 1-26.

Bartels, L. & Doverspike, D. (1997) Assessing the assessor: The relationship of assessor personality to leniency in assessment center ratings. *Journal of Social Behavior and Personality, 12*, 179-190.

Bartels, L. K., & Doverspike, D. (1997). Effects of disaggregation on managerial assessment center validity. *Journal of Business and Psychology, 12*, 45-53.

Binning, J. F., & Barrett, G. V. (1989). Validity of personnel decisions: A conceptual analysis of the inferential and evidential bases. *Journal of Applied Psychology, 74*, 478-494.

Campion, M. A., Pursell, E. D., & Brown, B. K. (1988). Structured interviewing: Raising the psychometric properties of the employment interview. *Personnel Psychology, 41*, 25-42.

Celek, T., Zander, D., & Kampert, P. (1996). *Inside the Soul of a New Generation: Insights and Strategies for Reaching Busters.* Grand Rapids, MI: Zondervan Publishing House.

Cellar, D. F., Miller, M. L., Doverspike, D., & Klausky, J. D. (1996). A comparison of factor structures and criterion-related validity coefficients for personality measures based on the lexical and questionnaire five-factor models: Effect of scale transparency on factor structure and prediction. *Journal of Applied Psychology, 81,* 694-704.

Coffee, K. (1998). Candidate reduction strategies. *Public Personnel Management, 27,* 459-473.

Coupland, D. (1991). *Generation X: Tales for an Accelerated Culture.* New York, NY: St. Martin's.

DiCaprio, N. S. (1974). *Personality Theories: Guides to Living.* Philadelphia, PA: Saunders.

Dipboye, R. L., & Gaugler, B. B. (1993). Cognitive and behavioral processes in the selection interview. In N. Schmitt & W. C. Borman (Eds.). *Personnel selection in organizations* (pp. 135-170). San Francisco, CA: Jossey-Bass.

Doverspike, D., Barrett, G. V., & Alexander, R. A. (1985). The feasibility of traditional validation procedures for demonstrating job relatedness. *Law and Psychology Review, 9,* 35-44.

Doverspike, D., Taylor, M. A., & Arthur, W. A., Jr. (1999). *Affirmative Action: A Psychological Perspective.* Commack, NY: Nova Scientific Press.

Edwards, A. L. (1959). *Edwards Personnel Preference Schedule.* New York: The Psychological Corporation.

Griggs V. Duke Power Company, 401 U.S. 424 (1971).

Hahn, T., & Verhaagen, D. (1996). Reckless Hope: Understanding and Reaching Baby Busters. Grand Rapids, MI: Baker Books.

Helms, J. E. (1983). A Practitioners Guide to the Edwards Personal Preference Schedule. Springfield, IL: Charles C. Thomas.

Highhouse, S., Beadle, D., Gallo, A., & Miller, L. (1998). Get em' while they last! Effects of scarcity information on job advertisements. Journal of Applied Social Psychology, 28, 779-795.

Highhouse, S., Zickar, M. J., Thorsteinson, T. J., Stierwalt, S. L., & Slaughter, J. E. (1999). Assessing company employment image: An example in the fast food industry. Personnel Psychology, 52, 151-172.

Hollis-Sawyer, L. & Doverspike D. (in press). Reasonable accommodation in the workplace: Implications of the ADEA and ADA for older workers. Journal of Ethics, Law and Aging.

Holtz, G. T. (1995). Welcome to the Jungle: The Why Behind "Generation X." New York: St Martin's Press.

Hough, L. M. (1984). Development and evaluation of the "Accomplishment record method of selecting and promoting professionals." Journal of Applied Psychology, 69, 135-146.

Jackson, M. (1999, January 31). Firms learn to cope with Generation X. The Plain Dealer, pp. 1-H, 5-H.

Latham, G. P., Saari, L. M. (1984). Do people do what they say? Further studies on the situational interview. Journal of Applied Psychology, 69, 569-573.

Latham, G. P., Saari, L. M., Pursell, E. D., & Campion, M. A. (1980). The situational interview. *Journal of Applied Psychology, 65,* 422-427.

Maslow, A. H. (1968). *Toward a Psychology of Being, Second Edition.* Princeton, NJ: Van Nostrand.

Maslow, A. H. (1971). *The Farther Reaches of Human Nature.* New York, NY: Viking.

McClelland, D. C. (1961). *The Achieving Society.* New York: Free Press.

Muchnick, M. (1996). *Naked Management: Bare Essentials for Motivating the X-Generation at Work.* Delray Beach, FL: St. Lucie Press.

Murray, H. A. (1938). *Explorations in Personality.* New York: Oxford.

Murray, H. A. (1943). *Thematic Apperception Test.* Cambridge, MA: Harvard.

Noe, R. A. (1999). *Employee Training & Development.* Boston, MA: McGraw-Hill.

Odiorne, G. S. (1981). *The Change Resisters: How They Prevent Progress and What Managers Can Do About Them.* Englewood Cliffs: Prentice Hall.

Pincus, L. B., & Belohlav, J. A. (1996). Legal issues in multinational business strategy: To play the game, you have to know the rules. *Academy of Management Executive, 10,* 52_61.

Raymark, P. H., Schmit, M. J., & Guion, R. M. (1997). Identifying potentially useful personality constructs for employee selection. *Personnel Psychology, 50,* 723-736.

Ritchie, K. (1995). *Marketing to Generation X.* New York: Lexington Books.

Robertson, I. T., Gratton, L., & Rout, U. (1990). The validity of situational interviews for administrative jobs. *Journal of Organizational Behavior*, 11, 69-76.

Rynes, S. L. (1993). When recruitment fails to attract: Individual expectations meet organizational realities in recruitment. In Schuler, H., Farr, H. L., & Smith, M. (Eds.). *Personnel Selection and Assessment: Individual and Organizational Perspectives*. Hillsdale, NJ: Lawrence Erlbaum (pp. 27-40).

Rynes, S. L., Orlitzky, M. O., & Bretz, R. D., Jr., (1997). Experience hiring versus college recruiting: Practices and emerging trends. *Personnel Psychology*, 50, 309-339.

Sidick, J. T., Barrett, G. V., & Doverspike, D. (1994). Three-alternative multiple choice tests: An attractive option. *Personnel Psychology*, 47, 829-835.

Schuler, H., Farr, H. L., & Smith, M. (Eds.). (1993). *Personnel Selection and Assessment: Individual and Organizational Perspectives*. Hillsdale, NJ: Lawrence Erlbaum.

Tulgan, B. (1995). *Managing Generation X: How to Bring Out the Best in Young Talent*. Santa Monica, California: Merritt Publishing.

Weekley, J. A., & Gier, J. A. (1987). Reliability and validity of the situational interview for a sales position. *Journal of Applied Psychology*, 72, 484-487.

Index

The Authors

Dennis Doverspike, Ph.D., ABPP, is a Full Professor of Psychology at the University of Akron and a Fellow of the Institute for Life-Span Development and Gerontology. He holds a Diplomate in Industrial/Organizational Psychology from the American Board of Professional Psychology. Currently, his major research interests include recruiting, compensation, diversity, and testing and assessment issues. He is a coauthor, with Mary Anne Taylor and Winfred Arthur, Jr., of the book *Affirmative Action: A Psychological Perspective*. He is also the author or coauthor of over 70 professional publications. His research has appeared in journals such as *Journal of Applied Psychology*, *Personnel Psychology*, *Journal of Business and Psychology* and *Public Personnel Management*.

Dennis Doverspike received his Ph.D. in Psychology in 1983 from the University of Akron. His M.S. in Psychology is from the University of Wisconsin-Oshkosh and his B.S. is from John Carroll University. From 1982 till 1984, he was a member of the psychology and graduate faculties at the University of Nebraska at Omaha. Since 1984, he has been a member of the psychology faculty at the University of Akron. He has taught courses at both the graduate and undergraduate levels, and directed dissertations, thesis and practica.

He is a member of Sigma Xi, the American Psychological Association, te Academy of Management, the American Psychological Society, the International Personnel Management Association, the Society for Human Resource Management, and the American Statistical Society. At the University of Akron, he serves as the faculty advisor to Psi Chi and the Psychology Club.

Dennis Doverspike can be reached by email at either ddoverspike@uakron.edu or DOORSDEN@aol.com.

Rhonda Charlene Tuel has a Bachelor's degree in Psychology from the University of Akron, Akron, Ohio, (1993) and is pursuing her Masters in Clinical Counseling at Walsh University, North Canton, Ohio. Since 1996, Ms. Tuel has been employed at Diebold, Inc., North Canton, Ohio, where she is responsible for the Human Resource Function for their Corporate Customer and Technology Support Center, which includes their worldwide call center and all levels of technical help desks. In addition, she is responsible for human resources in the Direct Marketing Operation.

Rhonda Tuel is a member of Who's Who, Omicron Delta Kappa National Leadership Honorary, Mortar Board Leadership Society, Psi Chi National Psychology Honorary, Pi Sigma Epsilon Professional Marketing Fraternity, Phi Eta Sigma Arts and Sciences Honorary, American Counseling Association, Society for Human Resource Management, Stark State University Advisory Board and Stark County Human Resource Society.

BUSINESS AND CAREER RESOURCES

Contact Impact Publications for a free annotated listing of resources or visit the World Wide Web for a complete listing of resources: www.impactpublications.com. The following books are available directly from Impact Publications. Complete the following form or list the titles, include postage (see formula at the end), enclose payment, and send your order to:

IMPACT PUBLICATIONS
9104 Manassas Drive, Suite N
Manassas Park, VA 20111-5211
Tel 1-800/361-1055, 703/361-7300, or Fax 703/335-9486
Quick and easy online ordering: *www.impactpublications.com*

Qty.	Titles	Price	Total
BOOKS BY RAY SCHREYER AND JOHN MCCARTER			
	The Best 100 Web Sites for HR Professionals	13.95	
	The Employer's Guide to Recruiting on the Internet	24.95	
	Recruit and Retain the Best	14.95	
THE CAREERSAVVY SERIES			
	100 Top Internet Job Sites	12.95	
	101 Hiring Mistakes Employers Make...Avoid Them	14.95	
	Anger and Conflict in the Workplace	15.95	
	The Best 100 Web Sites for HR Professionals	13.95	
	The Difficult Hire	14.95	
	Recruit and Retain the Best	14.95	
	Savvy Interviewing	10.95	
	The Savvy Resume Writer	12.95	
HIRING & RETENTION			
	45 Effective Ways for Hiring Smart!	24.95	
	96 Great Interview Questions to Ask Before You Hire	16.95	
	Ask the Right Questions, Hire the Best People	14.99	
	CareerXroads 2000	26.95	
	Complete Reference Checking Handbook	29.95	
	Directory of Executive Recruiters 2000	47.95	
	Employer's Guide to Recruiting on the Internet	24.95	
	Essential Book of Interviewing	15.00	
	Fast Forward MBA in Hiring	14.95	
	Finding and Keeping Great Employees	24.95	

142

Qty.	Titles	Price	Total
_____	High Impact Hiring	34.95	_____
_____	Hire With Your Head	29.95	_____
_____	Hiring: How to Find & Keep the Best People	12.99	_____
_____	Hiring and Managing Personnel Library	299.95	_____
_____	Love 'Em or Lose 'Em	17.95	_____
_____	Manager's Book of Questions	12.95	_____
_____	Smart Hiring	12.95	_____
_____	Smart Staffing	19.95	_____
_____	Unofficial Guide to Hiring & Firing Employees	16.00	_____
_____	Verify Those Credentials	19.95	_____
_____	Weddle's Guide to Employment Web-sites	21.95	_____

MOTIVATING & ENERGIZING YOUR WORKFORCE

Qty.	Titles	Price	Total
_____	1001 Ways to Energize Employees	12.00	_____
_____	1001 Ways to Reward Employees	12.00	_____
_____	A New Attitude	99.00	_____
_____	Attitude!	149.00	_____
_____	Bringing Out the Best in People	21.95	_____
_____	Dilbert Principle	20.00	_____
_____	Getting Employees to Fall in Love with Your Company	17.95	_____
_____	How to Be a Star at Work	12.00	_____
_____	Joy of Work	22.00	_____
_____	Motivating and Rewarding Employees	99.00	_____
_____	Motivation and Goal-Setting	99.00	_____
_____	Passionate Organization	24.95	_____
_____	Take This Job and Thrive	14.95	_____

INTERNET JOB SEARCH/HIRING

Qty.	Titles	Price	Total
_____	Career Exploration On the Internet	15.95	_____
_____	Electronic Resumes	19.95	_____
_____	Employer's Guide to Recruiting on the Internet	24.95	_____
_____	Guide to Internet Job Search.	14.95	_____
_____	Heart & Soul Internet Job Search	16.95	_____
_____	Internet Jobs Kit	149.95	_____
_____	Internet Resumes	14.95	_____
_____	Job Searching Online for Dummies	24.99	_____
_____	Resumes in Cyberspace	14.95	_____

ALTERNATIVE JOBS & EMPLOYERS

Qty.	Titles	Price	Total
_____	100 Best Careers for the 21st Century	15.95	_____
_____	100 Great Jobs and How To Get Them	17.95	_____
_____	101 Careers	16.95	_____
_____	150 Best Companies for Liberal Arts Graduates	15.95	_____
_____	50 Coolest Jobs in Sports	15.95	_____
_____	Adams Job Almanac 2000	16.95	_____
_____	American Almanac of Jobs and Salaries	20.00	_____
_____	Back Door Guide to Short-Term Job Adventures	19.95	_____
_____	Best Jobs for the 21st Century	19.95	_____
_____	Breaking & Entering	17.95	_____
_____	Careers in Computers	17.95	_____
_____	Careers in Health Care	17.95	_____

Qty.	Titles	Price	Total
_____	Careers in High Tech	17.95	_____
_____	Career Smarts	12.95	_____
_____	College Not Required	12.95	_____
_____	Cool Careers for Dummies	16.95	_____
_____	Cybercareers	24.95	_____
_____	Directory of Executive Recruiters	47.95	_____
_____	Flight Attendant Job Finder	16.95	_____
_____	Great Jobs Ahead	11.95	_____
_____	Health Care Job Explosion!	17.95	_____
_____	Hidden Job Market 2000	18.95	_____
_____	High-Skill, High-Wage Jobs	19.95	_____
_____	JobBank Guide to Computer and High-Tech Companies	16.95	_____
_____	JobSmarts Guide to Top 50 Jobs	15.00	_____
_____	Liberal Arts Jobs	14.95	_____
_____	Media Companies 2000	18.95	_____
_____	Quantum Companies II	26.95	_____
_____	Sunshine Jobs	16.95	_____
_____	Take It From Me	12.00	_____
_____	Top 100	19.95	_____
_____	Top 2,500 Employers 2000	18.95	_____
_____	Trends 2000	14.99	_____
_____	What Employers Really Want	14.95	_____
_____	Working in TV News	12.95	_____
_____	Workstyles to Fit Your Lifestyle	11.95	_____
_____	You Can't Play the Game If You Don't Know the Rules	14.95	_____

RECRUITERS/EMPLOYERS

Qty.	Titles	Price	Total
_____	Adams Executive Recruiters Almanac	16.95	_____
_____	Directory of Executive Recruiters 2000	47.95	_____
_____	Employer's Guide to Recruiting on the Internet	24.95	_____
_____	Job Seekers Guide to Executive Recruiters	34.95	_____
_____	Job Seekers Guide to Recruiters In. . .Series	36.95	_____

JOB STRATEGIES AND TACTICS

Qty.	Titles	Price	Total
_____	101 Ways to Power Up Your Job Search	12.95	_____
_____	110 Big Mistakes Job Hunters	19.95	_____
_____	24 Hours to Your Next Job, Raise, or Promotion	10.95	_____
_____	Better Book for Getting Hired	11.95	_____
_____	Career Bounce-Back	14.95	_____
_____	Career Chase	17.95	_____
_____	Career Fitness	19.95	_____
_____	Career Intelligence	15.95	_____
_____	Career Starter	10.95	_____
_____	Coming Alive From 9 to 5	18.95	_____
_____	Complete Idiot's Guide to Changing Careers	17.95	_____
_____	Executive Job Search Strategies	16.95	_____
_____	First Job Hunt Survival Guide	11.95	_____
_____	Five Secrets to Finding a Job	12.95	_____
_____	Get a Job You Love!	19.95	_____
_____	Get It Together By 30	14.95	_____
_____	Get the Job You Want Series	37.95	_____
_____	Get Ahead! Stay Ahead!	12.95	_____

Qty.	Titles	Price	Total
_____	Getting from Fired to Hired	14.95	_____
_____	Great Jobs for Liberal Arts Majors	11.95	_____
_____	How to Get a Job in 90 Days or Less	12.95	_____
_____	How to Get Interviews from Classified Job Ads	14.95	_____
_____	How to Succeed Without a Career Path	13.95	_____
_____	How to Get the Job You Really Want	9.95	_____
_____	How to Make Use of a Useless Degree	13.00	_____
_____	Is It Too Late To Run Away and Join the Circus?	14.95	_____
_____	Job Hunting in the 21st Century	17.95	_____
_____	Job Hunting for the Utterly Confused	14.95	_____
_____	Job Hunting Made Easy	12.95	_____
_____	Job Search: The Total System	14.95	_____
_____	Job Search Organizer	12.95	_____
_____	Job Search Time Manager	14.95	_____
_____	JobShift	13.00	_____
_____	JobSmart	12.00	_____
_____	Kiplinger's Survive and Profit From a Mid-Career Change	12.95	_____
_____	Knock 'Em Dead 2000	12.95	_____
_____	Me, Myself, and I, Inc.	17.95	_____
_____	New Rights of Passage	29.95	_____
_____	No One Is Unemployable	29.95	_____
_____	Not Just Another Job	12.00	_____
_____	Part-Time Careers	10.95	_____
_____	Perfect Job Search	12.95	_____
_____	Princeton Review Guide to Your Career	20.00	_____
_____	Perfect Pitch	13.99	_____
_____	Portable Executive	12.00	_____
_____	Professional's Job Finder	18.95	_____
_____	Reinventing Your Career	9.99	_____
_____	Resumes Don't Get Jobs	10.95	_____
_____	Right Fit	14.95	_____
_____	Right Place at the Right Time	11.95	_____
_____	Second Careers	14.95	_____
_____	Secrets from the Search Firm Files	24.95	_____
_____	So What If I'm 50	12.95	_____
_____	Staying in Demand	12.95	_____
_____	Strategic Job Jumping	13.00	_____
_____	SuccessAbilities	14.95	_____
_____	Take Yourself to the Top	13.99	_____
_____	Temping: The Insiders Guide	14.95	_____
_____	Top 10 Career Strategies for the Year 2000 & Beyond	12.00	_____
_____	Top 10 Fears of Job Seekers	12.00	_____
_____	Ultimate Job Search Survival	14.95	_____
_____	VGMs Career Checklist	9.95	_____
_____	Welcome to the Real World	13.00	_____
_____	What Do I Say Next?	20.00	_____
_____	What Employers Really Want	14.95	_____
_____	When Do I Start	11.95	_____
_____	Who Says There Are No Jobs Out There	12.95	_____
_____	Work Happy Live Healthy	14.95	_____
_____	Work This Way	14.95	_____
_____	You and Co., Inc.	22.00	_____
_____	Your Hidden Assets	19.95	_____

Qty.	Titles	Price	Total

TESTING AND ASSESSMENT

Qty.	Titles	Price	Total
_____	Career Counselor's Tool Kit	45.00	_____
_____	Career Discovery Project	12.95	_____
_____	Career Exploration Inventory	29.95	_____
_____	Career Satisfaction and Success	14.95	_____
_____	Career Tests	12.95	_____
_____	Crystal-Barkley Guide to Taking Charge of Your Career	9.95	_____
_____	Dictionary of Holland Occupational Codes	45.00	_____
_____	Discover the Best Jobs For You	14.95	_____
_____	Discover What You're Best At	12.00	_____
_____	Gifts Differing	14.95	_____
_____	Have You Got What It Takes?	12.95	_____
_____	How to Find the Work You Love	10.95	_____
_____	Making Vocational Choices	29.95	_____
_____	New Quick Job Hunting Map	4.95	_____
_____	P.I.E. Method for Career Success	14.95	_____
_____	Putting Your Talent to Work	12.95	_____
_____	Real People, Real Jobs	15.95	_____
_____	Self-Directed Search and Related Holland Career Materials	27.95	_____
_____	Self-Directed Search Form R Combination Package	74.00	_____
_____	Starting Out, Starting Over	14.95	_____
_____	Test Your IQ	6.95	_____
_____	Three Boxes of Life	18.95	_____
_____	Type Talk	11.95	_____
_____	WORKTypes	12.99	_____

ATTITUDE & MOTIVATION

Qty.	Titles	Price	Total
_____	Ways to Motivate Yourself	15.99	_____
_____	Change Your Attitude	15.99	_____
_____	Reinventing Yourself	18.99	_____

INSPIRATION & EMPOWERMENT

Qty.	Titles	Price	Total
_____	10 Stupid Things Men Do to Mess Up Their Lives	13.00	_____
_____	10 Stupid Things Women Do	12.00	_____
_____	101 Great Resumes	9.99	_____
_____	101 Simple Ways to Be Good to Yourself	12.95	_____
_____	Awaken the Giant Within	12.00	_____
_____	Beating Job Burnout	12.95	_____
_____	Big Things Happen When You Do the Little Things Right	15.00	_____
_____	Career Busters	10.95	_____
_____	Chicken Soup for the Soul Series	87.95	_____
_____	Do What You Love, the Money Will Follow	11.95	_____
_____	Doing It All Isn't Everything	19.95	_____
_____	Doing Work You Love	14.95	_____
_____	Emotional Intelligence	13.95	_____
_____	First Things First	23.00	_____
_____	Get What You Deserve	23.00	_____
_____	Getting Unstuck	11.99	_____
_____	If It's Going To Be, It's Up To Me	22.00	_____
_____	If Life Is A Game, These Are the Rules	15.00	_____

Qty.	Titles	Price	Total
_____	In Search of Values	8.99	_____
_____	Job/Family Challenge: A 9-5 Guide	12.95	_____
_____	Kick In the Seat of the Pants	11.95	_____
_____	Kiplinger's Taming the Paper Tiger	11.95	_____
_____	Life Skills	17.95	_____
_____	Love Your Work and SuccessWill Follow	12.95	_____
_____	Path, The	14.95	_____
_____	Personal Job Power	12.95	_____
_____	Power of Purpose	20.00	_____
_____	Seven Habits of Highly Effective People	14.00	_____
_____	Softpower	10.95	_____
_____	Stop Postponing the Rest of Your Life	9.95	_____
_____	Suvivor Personality	12.00	_____
_____	To Build the Life You Want, Create the Work You Love	10.95	_____
_____	Unlimited Power	12.00	_____
_____	Wake-Up Calls	18.95	_____
_____	Your Signature Path	24.95	_____

RESUMES & LETTERS

Qty.	Titles	Price	Total
_____	$110,000 Resume	16.95	_____
_____	100 Winning Resumes for $100,000+ Jobs	24.95	_____
_____	101 Best Resumes	10.95	_____
_____	101 More Best Resumes	11.95	_____
_____	101 Quick Tips for a Dynamite Resume	13.95	_____
_____	1500+ Key Words for 100,000+	14.95	_____
_____	175 High-Impact Resumes	10.95	_____
_____	Adams Resume Almanac/Disk	19.95	_____
_____	America's Top Resumes for America's Top Jobs	19.95	_____
_____	Asher's Bible of Exec.utive Resumes	29.95	_____
_____	Best Resumes for $75,000+ Executive Jobs	14.95	_____
_____	Best Resumes for Attorneys	16.95	_____
_____	Better Resumes in Three Easy Steps	12.95	_____
_____	Blue Collar and Beyond	8.95	_____
_____	Blue Collar Resumes	11.99	_____
_____	Building a Great Resume	15.00	_____
_____	Complete Idiot's Guide to Writing the Perfect Resume	16.95	_____
_____	Conquer Resume Objections	10.95	_____
_____	Creating Your High School Resume and Portfolio	13.90	_____
_____	Creating Your Skills Portfolio	10.95	_____
_____	Cyberspace Resume Kit	16.95	_____
_____	Damn Good Resume Guide	12.95	_____
_____	Dynamite Resumes	14.95	_____
_____	Edge Resume and Job Search Strategy	23.95	_____
_____	Electronic Resumes and Onlline Networking	13.99	_____
_____	Encyclopedia of Job-Winning Resumes	16.95	_____
_____	Gallery of Best Resumes	16.95	_____
_____	Gallery of Best Resumes for Two-Year Degree Graduates	16.95	_____
_____	Heart & Soul Resumes	15.95	_____
_____	High Impact Resumes and Letters	19.95	_____
_____	How to Prepare Your Curriculum Vitae	14.95	_____
_____	Just Resumes	11.95	_____
_____	New Perfect Resume	10.95	_____

Qty.	Titles	Price	Total
_____	Overnight Resume	12.95	_____
_____	Portfolio Power	14.95	_____
_____	Power Resumes	14.95	_____
_____	Prof. Resumes/Executives, Managers, & Other Administrators	19.95	_____
_____	Quick Resume and Cover Letter Book	12.95	_____
_____	Ready-To-Go Resumes	29.95	_____
_____	Resume Catalog	15.95	_____
_____	Resume Magic	18.95	_____
_____	Resume Power	12.95	_____
_____	Resume Pro	24.95	_____
_____	Resume Shortcuts	14.95	_____
_____	Resume Writing Made Easy	11.95	_____
_____	Resumes for High School Grads.	9.95	_____
_____	Resumes for the Over-50 Job Hunter	14.95	_____
_____	Resumes for Re-Entry	10.95	_____
_____	Resume Winners from the Pros	17.95	_____
_____	Resumes for Dummies	12.99	_____
_____	Resumes for the Health Care Professional	14.95	_____
_____	Resumes, Resumes, Resumes	9.99	_____
_____	Resumes That Knock 'Em Dead	10.95	_____
_____	Resumes That Will Get You the Job You Want	12.99	_____
_____	Savvy Resume Writer	10.95	_____
_____	Sure-Hire Resumes	14.95	_____
_____	Winning Resumes	10.95	_____
_____	Wow! Resumes	63.95	_____
_____	Your First Resume	9.99	_____
_____	Your Resume	24.95	_____

COVER LETTERS

_____	101 Best Cover Letters	11.95	_____
_____	175 High-Impact Cover Letters	10.95	_____
_____	200 Letters for Job Hunters	19.95	_____
_____	201 Winning Cover Letters for the $100,000+ Jobs	24.95	_____
_____	201 Dynamite Job Search Letters	19.95	_____
_____	201 Killer Cover Letters	16.95	_____
_____	Complete Idiot's Guide to the Perfect Cover Letters	14.95	_____
_____	Cover Letters, Cover Letters, Cover Letters	9.99	_____
_____	Cover Letters for Dummies	12.99	_____
_____	Cover Letters that Knock 'Em Dead	10.95	_____
_____	Cover Letters That Will Get You the Job You Want	12.99	_____
_____	Dynamite Cover Letters	14.95	_____
_____	Gallery of Best Cover Letters	18.95	_____
_____	Haldane's Best Cover Letters for Professionals	15.95	_____
_____	Perfect Cover Letter	10.95	_____
_____	Winning Cover Letters	10.95	_____

ETIQUETTE AND IMAGE

_____	Business Etiquette and Professionalism	10.95	_____
_____	Dressing Smart in the New Millennium	15.95	_____
_____	Executive Etiquette in the New Workplace	14.95	_____
_____	First Five Minutes	14.95	_____
_____	John Molloy's Dress for Success (For Men)	13.99	_____

Qty.	Titles	Price	Total
_____	Lions Don't Need to Roar	10.99	_____
_____	New Professional Image	12.95	_____
_____	New Women's Dress for Success	12.99	_____
_____	Red Socks Don't Work	14.95	_____
_____	Successful Style	17.95	_____
_____	VGMs Complete Guide to Career Etiquette	12.95	_____
_____	Winning Image	17.95	_____
_____	You've Only Got 3 Seconds	22.95	_____

INTERVIEWING: JOBSEEKERS

Qty.	Titles	Price	Total
_____	101 Dynamite Answers to Interview Questions	12.95	_____
_____	101 Dynamite Questions to Ask at Your Job Interview	14.95	_____
_____	101 Tough Interview Questions. . .	14.95	_____
_____	111 Dynamite Ways to Ace Your Job Interview	13.95	_____
_____	Best Answers/201 Most Frequently Asked Interview Questions	10.95	_____
_____	Complete Q & A Job Interview Book	14.95	_____
_____	Conquer Interview Objectives	10.95	_____
_____	Get Hired	14.95	_____
_____	Haldane's Best Answers to Tough Interview Questions	15.95	_____
_____	Information Interviewing	10.95	_____
_____	Interview for Success	15.95	_____
_____	Interview Strategies That Will Get You the Job You Want	12.99	_____
_____	Interview Power	12.95	_____
_____	Job Interviews for Dummies	12.99	_____
_____	Job Interviews That Mean Business	12.00	_____
_____	Killer Interviews	10.95	_____
_____	Savvy Interviewer	10.95	_____
_____	Successful Interviewing for College Seniors	11.95	_____
_____	Sweaty Palms	8.95	_____
_____	Your First Interview	9.95	_____

NETWORKING

Qty.	Titles	Price	Total
_____	52 Ways to Re-Connect, Follow Up, and Stay in Touch	14.95	_____
_____	Dig Your Well Before You're Thirsty	24.95	_____
_____	Dynamite Networking for Dynamite Jobs	15.95	_____
_____	Dynamite Tele-Search	12.95	_____
_____	Effective Networking	10.95	_____
_____	Golden Rule of Schmoozing	12.95	_____
_____	Great Connections	11.95	_____
_____	How to Work a Room	11.99	_____
_____	Network Your Way to Success	19.95	_____
_____	Networking for Everyone	16.95	_____
_____	People Power	14.95	_____
_____	Power Networking	14.95	_____
_____	Power Schmoozing	12.95	_____
_____	Power To Get In	24.95	_____

SALARY NEGOTIATIONS

Qty.	Titles	Price	Total
_____	Dynamite Salary Negotiations	15.95	_____
_____	Get a Raise in 7 Days	14.95	_____
_____	Get More Money on Your Next Job	14.95	_____
_____	Negotiate Your Job Offer	14.95	_____

Qty.	Titles	Price	Total

ENTREPRENEURS AND CONSULTANTS

Qty.	Titles	Price	Total
_____	10 Hottest Consulting Practices	27.95	_____
_____	101 Best Businesses to Start	17.50	_____
_____	101 Best Home Businesses	14.99	_____
_____	101 Best Weekend Businesses	14.99	_____
_____	555 Ways to Earn Extra Money	12.95	_____
_____	Adams Businesses You Can Start Almanac	14.95	_____
_____	Adams Streetwise Small Business Start-Up	16.95	_____
_____	Adams Streetwise Small Business Start-Up CD-ROM	59.95	_____
_____	Be Your Own Business	12.95	_____
_____	Best Home-Based Businesses for the 90s	12.95	_____
_____	Consultant's Proposal, Fee, and Contract Problem-Solver	19.95	_____
_____	Discovering Your Career in Business (With Disk)	22.00	_____
_____	Finding Your Perfect Work	16.95	_____
_____	Franchise Opportunities Handbook	16.95	_____
_____	Getting Business to Come to You CD-ROM	49.95	_____
_____	How to Raise a Family and Career Under One Roof	15.95	_____
_____	How to Really Start Your Own Business	19.95	_____
_____	How to Start, Run, and Stay in Business	14.95	_____
_____	Howto Succeed as an Independent Consultant	29.95	_____
_____	How to Start and Run a Successful Consulting Business	15.95	_____
_____	Ideal Entrepreneurial Business For You	16.95	_____
_____	Joining the Entrepreneurial Elite	25.95	_____
_____	NBEW's Guide to Self-Employment	12.95	_____
_____	Selling on the Internet	24.95	_____
_____	Start-Up	16.99	_____
_____	Starting on a Shoestring	16.95	_____
_____	Winning Government Contracts	19.95	_____

☞ **SUBTOTAL** $ _____

☞ Virginia residents add 4°% sales tax) _____

☞ Shipping/handling, Continental U.S., $5.00 + _____ $5.00
plus following percentages when **SUBTOTAL** is:
❏ $30-$100—multiply SUBTOTAL by 8% _____
❏ $100-$999—multiply SUBTOTAL by 7% _____
❏ $1,000-$4,999—multiply SUBTOTAL by 6% _____
❏ Over $5,000—multiply SUBTOTAL by 5% _____

☞ ❏ If shipped outside Continental US, add another 5% _____

☞ **TOTAL ENCLOSED** $ _____

SHIP TO: (street address only for UPS or RPS delivery)

Name _____

Address _____

_____

_____

Telephone _____

I enclose o Check o Money Order in the amount of: $ _____

Charge $ _____ to ❏ Visa ❏ MC ❏ AmEx

Card # _____ Exp: _____ / _____

Signature _____

The Click and Easy™ Online Career Resource Centers –

Books, videos, software, training materials, articles, and advice for job seekers, employers, HR professionals, schools, and libraries

Visit us online for all your career needs:

www.impactpublications.com
(career superstore and Impact)

www.winningthejob.com
(articles and advice)

www.veteransworld.com
(military transition)